Stewards

of the

House

Stewards of the House:

The Detective Fiction

of Jonathan Latimer

Bill Brubaker

Library of Congress Catalogue Card No: 92-75452

ISBN: 0-87972-610-5 clothbound
      0-87972-611-3 paperback

Cover design by Gary Dumm and Laura Darnell-Dumm

Contents

Acknowledgments

I wish to state my appreciation to several: To Jo Ann Hanzlik Latimer, wife of the the late Jonathan Wyatt Latimer, for endorsing this project. To Jonathan Peabody Latimer, the executor of his father's literary estate, for help in establishing biographical and bibliographical facts and critically reading portions of the manuscript.

I wish also to thank: Charlotte Sommer, Office of Alumni Affairs, Knox College, for her generous aid in providing biographical records. Andy Jaysnovitch for providing scarce issues of *The Not So Private Eye*. The kind staff of Inter-Library Loan, Strozier Library, Florida State University. The Research Committee, Department of English, Florida State University, for funds in support of this project.

Latimer Chronology

1906   October 23. Jonathan Wyatt Latimer born in Chicago, Illinois, only child of Evelyn Wyatt and Jonathan Guy Latimer. The christened name Jonathan honors an ancestor attached to George Washington's staff during the Revolutionary War.

1922-25   Receives preparatory education at Mesa (Arizona) Ranch School.

1926-29   Completes A.B. (English major) at Knox College (Galesburg, Illinois), where he graduates Phi Beta Kappa. Spends summer of graduation bicycling around France and Germany.

1929-34   Reporter for the Chicago *Herald-Examiner* and *Chicago Tribune*.

1935   Staff editor, Publicity Department, Department of the Interior. *Murder in the Madhouse. Headed for a Hearse.*

1936-37   Residence in Key West. *The Lady in the Morgue. The Search for My Great-Uncle's Head* (new Peter Coffin series). To Universal Studios sells movie rights to first three William Crane novels. Marries Ellen Peabody, December 11, 1937.

1938-42   Moves to La Jolla, California, his city of residence for the remainder of his life. Continues and concludes William Crane series with *The Dead Don't Care* (1938) and *Red Gardenias* (1939). Writes African adventure novel *Dark Memory* (1940) and continues detective fiction with *Solomon's Vineyard* (1941). Writes film scripts for five movies produced by Columbia, M.G.M., United Artists, Paramount, including *The Glass Key* based on Dashiell Hammett's novel.

1942-45   Serves in the U.S. Navy as executive officer on a destroyer assigned to convoy duty in the Atlantic and Mediterranean.

1946-59   Returns to La Jolla and reenters film writing career,

iii

scripting or co-scripting 15 films for RKO, Paramount, Warner Brothers, and Universal Studios, including the *film noir* classics *The Big Clock* and *The Night Has a Thousand Eyes*. Marries Jo Ann Hanzlik, December 18, 1954. Writes detective mysteries *Sinners and Shrouds* (1955) and *Black Is the Fashion for Dying* (1959).

1960-65   Writes 45 original scripts and adapts 50 Erle Stanley Gardner novels for Perry Mason television series.

1983   Dies June 23 of lung cancer at age 76.

Chapter 1
Person and Persona:
A Reading of Biography

As a reporter for the *Herald-Examiner* and *Chicago Tribune*, Jonathan Wyatt Latimer found himself at the center of polarities of private experience and national history upon entering the working world in the Depression autumn of 1929. In the house on Madison Avenue (the *Herald-Examiner*) and his boyhood home there lived mentors and patriarchs who required satisfaction, held him to standards at a time when social and economic collapse threatened. Born in Chicago as the only child to a family in comfortable circumstances and tracing its roots to Revolutionary origins, he grew toward his profession as a writer in a city of diverse ethnic neighborhoods populated by children of slaves from the American South, by Irish, Italian, German, Greek, and Polish immigrants, and by those of Jewish, mainline Protestant, born-again Fundamentalist, Catholic, and Greek Orthodox faiths. Such diversity of itself was sufficient to generate conflict in the political and business life of the city, where each new group made another minority struggling for political power, work, and wealth. But it was also a time when Chicago as an industrial and investment center suffered from the exhaustion of the depressed 1930s' economy, and the fear of unemployment hung over the city and seems never to have been remote from the writer's consciousness. Add to this the city's unfortunate history that connected crime and politics in the post-Prohibition hangover of gangsterism, and it is not difficult to understand how this Chicago so readily served as the landscape of violence and criminality in many of Latimer's detective novels.

That was the Chicago he experienced as a reporter. Starting with the Hearst *Herald-Examiner*, he was most often assigned to cover police precincts, and his reporting dealt mostly with

criminal matters: gangland slayings, kidnappings, more or less routine homicides, race riots, bank embezzlements and such. I knew Al Capone, George "Bugs" Moran and assorted other gangsters, as well as whorehouse madams, pimps, dope peddlers and con men. Later I became a rewrite man, taking stories from reporters by telephone and putting them into proper shape. One Sunday, when I was the only rewrite man in the *Herald-Examiner* office, I established some sort of record by writing about ten thousand words in six hours about the machine-gun slaying of Chicago's second most prominent union labor boss on his way home from church and the escape of John Dillinger, at the time the country's most notorious outlaw, from the Crown Point, Indiana, jail. (Latimer, Interview, *Megavore* 16)[1]

However, it was a safer, more advantageous and orthodox city to which Latimer was born on October 23, 1906, the son of Evelyn Wyatt and Jonathan Guy Latimer. His given name Jonathan Wyatt suggests the strength of tradition, the pride in family identity which incorporated his mother's surname with the Jonathan that was his father's name as well as a name recurrent in family history from the time of Colonel Jonathan Latimer, an aide to General Washington and associate of Nathan Hale. (The name Jonathan continues through the writer's conferring it upon his own second child.) In the course of his life, the detective novelist took an interest in gathering genealogical information about the Latimer family; and in the same way that his series detective preferred William rather than Bill Crane, the writer's choice of pen name was always Jonathan Latimer rather than the Jack otherwise informally used (Latimer, Letter to author).

The resources of Latimer's parents provided an education that predicted success. The years 1922-1925 saw him attend the Mesa (Arizona) Ranch School (later known as Valley Ranch School), an undenominational college preparatory school for boys. Its principals were a Cambridge M.A. and Harvard A.B.; its staff of five taught 25 boys; it offered a special tutoring camp in the spring months of each year for the College Boards in June. Each boy was assigned a tent house and a horse for which he had sole responsibility. Facilities existed for tennis, swimming, basketball, and billiards. Photographs of the school during Latimer's tenure show cadets in a military camp; they wear army cavalry uniforms and stand at attention before their tenthouses as a bugler calls for inspection. Mesa Ranch School seems to have emphasized the traditional core of academic subjects and a life designed to promote strong male character as it was then conventionally understood (*Handbook* 540, 817). A humorous reference to the school occurs in *The Dead Don't Care* (1938) when the detective William Crane notes that it was the last in the line of several prep schools from which the decadent Penn Essex (certainly of a lesser discipline than Latimer) was expelled (*Dead* 26).

Following his graduation from Mesa Ranch School, it seemed fated that Latimer should attend Knox College and become the third generation of Latimer males to be schooled there. Southwest of Chicago in Galesburg, the private co-educational liberal arts college drew children of middle and upper-class families from the state and region. An examination of the school annuals during Latimer's junior and senior years reflect cultural homogeneity in the student body, which appears to have been mostly white, Christian, and of Anglo-European origin. Latimer as a Knox student was a tall, attractive person of dark hair and regular features with a pleasant, muted smile; one who dressed even more neatly than his contemporaries at a time when persons of his social class generally turned out looking rather well for photographic sessions. The caption accompanying his junior year photograph observes that "Jack has the [k]nack of knowing all about everything without any visible effort."

As an English major, his record was excellent, with special strength in classics and philosophy, and he graduated with membership in the Friars (men's honorary), Key Club, and Phi Beta Kappa. No drudge, his activities reflected multiple interests: activity in the social fraternity Phi Delta Theta, intramural sports, "K" Council (letterman's club), and yearbook staff and manager of the homecoming show for 1929. As athlete he chose neither the football nor basketball that Knox offered, but tennis and golf, games of individual performance that have traditional association with middle and upper-class life. He performed especially well in golf, winning the state collegiate golf tournaments during three of his undergraduate years.[1]

The immediate reward for completing the A.B. so meritoriously was a vacation spent bicycling around France and Germany in the summer of 1929. (There is probably an echo of this experience in *The Dead Don't Care,* in which the dancer Imago Paraguay's cosmeticed face reminds William Crane of a "painted death mask of an Egyptian princess he had once seen in a Berlin museum. He had gone into the museum thinking it was his hotel" [96].)

But summer vacation was over and in October 1929, the young man would turn 23. Then what? A time of hard choices for any graduate and especially in the dark autumn weeks of the collapsed stock market and the beginning of the Great Depression. Latimer's college achievements give a picture of one likely to assume a career in government, business, or one of the professions, perhaps the academic life. The student's success in literature, classics, and philosophy could easily have served as entry into graduate study and the career of a professor, like that of his amateur detective Peter Coffin in *The Search for My Great-Uncle's Head* (1937). His own father, the Jonathan before him, was a lawyer who had connections with political life in Washington and maintained a successful practice in a partnership on Chicago's South LaSalle Street.

So what was the sole child, the male Jonathan son of Jonathan son of the ur-Jonathans to do in the dark autumn of 1929? In retirement the writer remembered no uncertainty. As a child he had always been an omnivorous reader of "wildly diverse writers ranging from whoever wrote Tom Swift and The Rover Boys to Dumas, Dickens, Victor Hugo, etc. and I dreamed of being one of them as other kids dreamed of being baseball or football stars" (*Megavore* 16).

Toward that end he accepted his first employment, the job as a staff reporter on *The Herald-American*. The apprenticeship to writing served through newspaper journalism is a history repeated among the canonized American writers: Franklin, Whitman, Twain, Howells, Crane, Hemingway. Latimer himself saw newspaper work as "one of the best training schools for would-be writers, requiring clarity, brevity and self-discipline" (*Megavore* 16), a judgment echoed in Hemingway's evaluation of his own journalistic experience. In his account of the *Herald* during Latimer's time, George Murray records the detective novelist's name as well as those of the dramatist Charles McArthur and the film writers Jo Swerling and Wallace Smith as writers-made-good whose apprenticeship in the vast ugly quarters of the newspaper building on Madison Street prepared them for their careers (Murray 299).

However, dynamics other than the wishful dream of profession and the practical development of writing skill were working in Latimer as he job-shifted from the *Herald* to the *Chicago Tribune* and on to the Publicity Department of the Federal Department of the Interior. The possibility of failure must never have been remote from his consciousness. It was a decade when failure for most meant unemployment, a fear Latimer's William Crane suffers recurrently in the series novels as the agency detective worries that his job performance may not please his boss sufficiently for retention.

In the writer's private life, failure as newspaper journalist or as novelist would not likely have meant economic disaster, given the resources of the family; but it would have violated the code of success by which Latimer males lived. There seems little doubt that the writer's successful father wished success upon the son, influenced him toward it, and tried to manage events to make it happen. This is demonstrated in both small and large ways. At Knox College it was the father who required the son to play the golf by which the undergrad won three state championships. The father's commission in Chicago as a lawyer for the National Recovery Administration under Secretary of the Interior Harold Ickes must have entered into the son's further job shift from the *Chicago Tribune* to a new position as a staff writer working with Ickes in the Department of the Interior. In response to a request for information from Knox College about his son's writing career, the father's pride swells as he lists his son's first successes for a centennial directory of distinguished alumnus.

No doubt the writer-son took pleasure in satisfying the expectations of his father. His Knox College record was, after all, formidable assurance that he could do that. But at times he seems to have felt a bit pushed, if not put out, by the efforts of his senior, though it would be erroneous to believe that anything so strong as a rift existed between Jonathan Wyatt and his parents. Still, after satisfying them at Knox College with his superiority in golf, which his father required him to play, he vowed after graduation never to play the game again and in his own family was never known to do so, though he retained his interest in tennis to the end of his life.

And the father's enthusiastic response to the alumni office request for information gives a picture of the writer's discomfort with bearing the load the senior Latimer placed upon him. The son having failed to answer an earlier query, his father sought to explain the writer's lapse: "Jack doesn't respond to any publicity-questionnaire and there isn't any use in forwarding blanks to him." Therefore Jonathan Guy would provide what the son would not, including the promotional and inaccurate statement that Jonathan Wyatt was the "Author of three Detective novels the last one listed as a 'best seller' and the last two now being dramatized for stage and movie production." Evidently chastised by the son, the father substituted more restrained words in another letter, urging that the citation of the writer's activities be confined to "the statement that he is the author of 3 Detective Novels—[for] Jack and I would be greatly displeased if irrelevant and self advertising information was used in this connection..." (Latimer, Letter...undated; Latimer, Letter to Knox).[2]

6 Stewards of the House

The son's correcting of the father is suggestive. Chafing under patriarchal authority, the writer possessed feelings of ambivalence about living under the long gaze of the Fathers, enjoying growth under their scrutiny but sometimes struggling to maintain his sense of selfhood, always conscious of the Gaze taking his measure.

In 1935 Jonathan Latimer moved from his reporter's job with the *Chicago Tribune* to a position as staff editor in the Publicity Department of the Department of Interior. He first met the head of the department, Harold Ickes, in the course of an assignment from the *Trib*, which saw him covering the official's visit to the city on the occasion of a political speech. In Latimer's account of the experience, his editor had ordered him "to put the needle in Ickes" since

The Tribune wasn't exactly sympathetic to the administration. I did a pretty good needle job, but when Ickes saw the story he said it was the best thing that had ever been written about him, so he hired me as ghost writer and doubled my salary. (Latimer, Interview…Scarr)

Working for Ickes gave Latimer another experience of mentoring under a successful, experienced senior male. Although Secretary Ickes liked being known to the world through the benign nickname of "Honest Harold," with his associates he was recognized for his caustic and demanding personal style. As head of the Department of the Interior, he administered several of the far-flung programs of President Roosevelt's New Deal, the effort toward economic renewal instituted through the National Recovery Administration and the Public Works Administration, both of which functioned through a network of associated federal agencies in state and regional offices. (It was for the Chicago office of the N.R.A., for example, that Latimer's father had a commission to carry out legal work.)

The organization of the work done by the Department of the Interior would have appeared not unlike that of newspaper work as the writer had known it in Chicago. There, a hierarchy of office delegated the work downward from publishers to chief editors to editors of desks to rewrite editors to reporters. In the Department of Interior it was department to agency to bureau to field office, with each its own cadre of managers and employees, the large difference between Chicago newspaper and Washington department of government being that of scope. The organization of the Department was also not unlike that of an industrial corporation. For chairman and board substitute President and Congress; for CEO substitute Secretary of the Department; for heads of divisions substitute agency chiefs, and so on. In all these organizational patterns, the abstractions of purpose are translated into product produced by labor under the direction of middle managers, the sort of position occupied by Latimer as rewrite editor and ghostwriter.

Latimer's major assignment during his tenure in Washington was the ghostwriting of a book published under Secretary Ickes' name: *Back to Work: The Story of the P.W.A.* (1935). For Latimer the process of its writing was a further experience of departmental structure and the managerial organization of work. Clark Foreman, on loan to Secretary Ickes from the Rosenwald Foundation as a dollar-a-year man, developed the plan for generating its materials. Summary reports, statistics, and graphs were prepared in the field by directors of divisions and submitted upward to another editor, Michael Ross, after whose work Latimer held the assignment to prepare the final rewriting of the manuscript.

The publication of the book under Harold Ickes' name drew criticism from the *Chicago Tribune,* which published a fierce attack upon the book and its author, charging that Ickes meant to pocket the royalties from its sale, had misused federal employees, and failed to give proper credit to its true authors. Given the anti-New Deal position of the newspaper and its publisher Colonel Robert McCormick, such a charge is not surprising, but Ickes felt stung. In fact, in the preface to *Back to Work*, the Secretary had given credit to its editors by name, and he had always meant to direct royalty payments toward use by the P.W.A. Recording a private defense Ickes argued that *Back to Work* was his book because he had followed it from its inception, its ideas were his own, and he had personally contributed to its editing.[4]

His service to Secretary Ickes completed, Latimer felt the months spent in Washington had been quite enough. His experience had given him a direct impression of how the machinery of government sought change, and how politics and personality factored in. In *The Dead Don't Care* (1938) William Crane seems to represent Latimer himself when the detective speaks coolly of the national capitol. To Department of Justice agent Wilson's apparent invitation to seek employment in the agency, Crane snubs him by responding indifferently that he never goes there (233). But whatever the writer's retrospective assessment of official life, the year had given him the opportunity to complete the manuscripts of two series novels, *Murder in the Madhouse* and *Headed for a Hearse,* and see their publication through the Crime Club division of Doubleday, Doran.

As suggested by the example above, the series detective William Crane embodies much of his creator's sensibility and experience. He holds perspectives in common with his creator: a sense of the past which invests the present with the standards of the older upper class, the heightened consciousness of living under the scrutiny of the Fathers, the desire to unite self with class by demonstrating merit to a father-mentor. The detective's anxiety about placating authority and maintaining his own identity—particularly as revealed in his efforts to certify his intelligence and practical ability in the resolution of assigned cases—recurs through the five narratives. His mentor, Colonel Black, seems to have uncanny prescience when Crane telephones or cables him about the progress of a case, as if the Colonel in his remote offices in the Chrysler Building were present to events, a hovering spirit, like the senior males in the writer's life: the *Urvater* Colonel Jonathan Latimer, father Jonathan Guy, publisher Colonel McCormick of the *Chicago Tribune,* the colonel-like Harold Ickes and the real colonels from the Army Corps of Engineers who headed offices in the Department of the Interior.

Buoyed by the prospect of further success with the Crane novels, Latimer cut his ties with Chicago and Washington and moved to Key West, where he remained through the years 1936 and 1937. County seat of Monroe County, the small city was struggling for survival after its bankruptcy in 1934 brought it under the control of the Federal Emergency Relief Administration.[5] Known for its sports fishing and cruise facilities, the Key West of that decade had in modest ways become commodified as a site of tourist industry attracting the wealthy. Aside from winter tourism it was a commercial fishing town, shipping port, naval base, and artists colony attractive to writers for its cheap living and relaxed tropical character, with pleasant mild weather through late fall, winter, and early spring, and plenty of hot summer days, to be sure, but usually with an ocean breeze of some kind. In certain narrow streets were cottages built in the previous century by small tradesmen and naval stores warehousemen in an architectural style suggestive of the houses in the New England ports from which their builders came. Other broader streets were lined with the high-ceilinged, two and three-storied houses of shipmasters and bankers, some in the Bahamian style with roof-shaded galleries on each floor and multiple doors and windows opening to the air.

Latimer lived not far from the city cemetery in a newer street of plain houses, occupying a cottage at 1218 Margaret Street, several blocks from Ernest Hemingway's grander house on Whitehead Street. In Key West, Latimer continued to develop the William Crane series. *Lady in the Morgue* (1936) maintains the Chicago setting of police precincts, Cook County morgue, hotels, streets, and hangouts the writer knew from his newspaper days. However, the novel's two cemetery scenes, with their descriptions of stone crypts and mausoleum entombments, suggest that the writer's mental image is a cemetery of surface burials like the one he passed by each day on Margaret Street. In his next Key West book, *The Search for My Great-Uncle's Head* (1937), Latimer introduced the amateur detective Peter Coffin in what was meant to be the first mystery of a new series. But in the following *The Dead Don't Care* (1938) he returned to William Crane and made direct use of the Florida setting—Key Largo, Miami, the Overseas Highway, Key West, and the Straits of Florida—in the development of the narrative.

The writer enjoyed the island life for its tropical flavor and the classes of people who were attracted to it. A rather gregarious person, he made friends and acquaintances easily among both the writers who lived on the island and its winter tourists, one of whom, Ellen Peabody, was to become his wife. Responding to a review editor for information about his impressions of the place, he wrote enthusiastically of carrying out his vocation in such a grand natural environment, of tarpon fishing, tennis, even officiating as one of the judges of a Fourth of July beauty contest (Marx).[6]

There was also his heady success: continuing to place his novels with the Crime Club division of Doubleday, Doran, whose editors were enthusiastic about the new Peter Coffin series; contracting with *Collier's* magazine for serializations; and pulling off the coup of selling three of the William Crane novels to Universal Studios as vehicles for the actor Preston Foster.[7] For Latimer, a high dollar mark occurred upon the occasion of the agreements with Universal and *Collier's*, for which he received $19,000 (Latimer, Interview...Scarr).

Latimer always knew himself as a writer of a popular genre, taking pride in his craft and profession without pretentiousness. During Latimer's Florida residence, an episode occurred in the relationship between himself, Ernest Hemingway, and James T. Farrell that reflected among them conflicts basic to such issues as the search for audience, the choice of genre, and the social role of writers. In Key West to visit Hemingway, Farrell in fact lived with Latimer, who sometimes accommodated house guests when Ernest and Pauline Hemingway had no space. Although the three writers shared the Chicago area as their common origin, each held different conceptions of literary purpose. To Farrell, Latimer's work seemed lightweight stuff in the depression decade to one whose concern about social issues had produced such novels as *The Young Manhood of Studs Lonigan* (1935), the story of a young man's moral collapse in his contact with the Chicago underworld. While his *Note on Literary Criticism* (1936) offers a critique of both the political left and right, its socialist perspective is clear.

Then there was Hemingway, at this point engaged in writing his own tough-guy novel *To Have and Have Not* (1937) and continuing an idiosyncratic program as a writer of fiction marked by the times but not otherwise readily contained by labels. To Rexford Guy Tugwell, a member of President Roosevelt's Brain Trust and a winter visitor to Key West in 1936, Ernest Hemingway did not seem to possess a thorough understanding of, or much sympathy for, the efforts toward national renewal set going by the New Deal. As reported by Carlos Baker in his biography of the writer, when Tugwell tried to interest Hemingway in politics as a worthy subject for fiction, the writer dismissed such a focus as of little interest (297).

Latimer professed to admire Hemingway and his art. In two interviews (one within a few years of his Key West life, another from the distance of age), the detective fiction writer noted their friendship and acknowledged the artist's influence upon the style of his own narratives (Latimer, "There's" 371).[8] If he had searched for confirmation of that admiration in Latimer's work, Hemingway would have been hard pressed to find them in the allusions to the famous Hemingwayesque lifestyle that occur in two of Latimer's novels. In *Murder in the Madhouse*, published before the two writers met, detective Crane stands at a mirror to assess facial wounds from an assault; he "thought he looked like Ernest Hemingway, only smarter" (37). In *The Dead Don't Care* a scene takes place in Hemingway's favored Key West bar, Sloppy Joe's. Eager for clues to recover the kidnapped Camelia Essex, the detective overhears a conversation between two fishing captains and the bartender about a vessel from which a man was seen in the unsporting destruction of gaffed sailfish with a machine gun. The three argue about whether it was

"Ernest," the bartender insisting that "Ernest only uses the Tommy gun on sharks" (176). If Latimer admired the art of the man, his ad hominem humor in these references seems to work at the expense of the code of masculine behavior for which tough Ernest was known.

All this gives perspective upon Latimer's writing career as the subject of a conversation between Hemingway and Farrell. In the winter months of 1936 the two had developed a friendship of some warmth and confidentiality, at least as it was viewed by Farrell. Hemingway's biographer notes:

Farrell gave [Latimer] a public tongue-lashing for putting on literary airs. Ernest, who was present, took Farrell aside. "Jesus Christ, Jim," he said, "don't do that. Those fellows have nothing but their writing. Take that away from them and they'll commit suicide." (297)

When Carlos Baker's account of the event appeared in excerpt in the *Atlantic*, Latimer angrily responded with a letter to the editor, denying that the event ever occurred:

Farrell never gave me a public tongue-lashing for putting on literary airs, as Baker asserts. He never gave me a tongue-lashing for anything. What he did in Key West in 1936 was live with me.

The Hemingways occasionally used my place as a sort of annex for house visitors they either couldn't or didn't want to take care of. Farrell was one of these. He occupied my spare bedroom, ate my food, drank my liquor, and finally departed, saying neither thank you nor good-bye.

Baker's picture of me as a fatuous nonentity is a real hard putdown. I'd be crushed if it weren't for the London *Sunday Times*. In a fairly recent compilation of the world's greatest crime stories, its editor selected one that was being written in Key West that same year: *The Lady in the Morgue* by a man named Jonathan Latimer. (30-32)

It may be that this history of strife reflects only the clash of personality likely when successful, competing writers make contact in such a closed environment as Key West. The failed etiquette generating the antipathy between Farrell and Latimer is clear enough: Farrell wasn't a gracious guest; Latimer didn't like being bad-mouthed. Maybe Hemingway didn't like to be bad-mouthed either, if he knew of Latimer's fictional references to his macho posturing. But the judgment of Latimer by Farrell and Hemingway goes beyond manners. In the hierarchy of forms neither placed high value on the genre by which the mystery writer was achieving success. And maybe it distressed them that a pop lit writer should be doing so well, as Latimer indisputably was. That appears to be the sense of Farrell's condemnation of Latimer for "putting on literary airs" and Hemingway's implying that "fellows" like Latimer have little stock beyond their short moment. Or at least so the writer perceived the comments, as Latimer's defense in the *Atlantic* letter makes certain; for there he cites the detached judgment of the venerable *Times* as certification that his books did possess merit, and the Florida residence was certainly a marked period of success.

But betrothal and the beckoning of new career possibilities in California terminated Latimer's residence in Key West. His final weeks there were marked by activities surrounding his marriage to Ellen Peabody, whom he'd met when she visited the island. The two shared a common identity by class and education. Of the Detroit social elite, Ellen Peabody had attended Grosse Pointe Country Day School and graduated from Miss Porter's finishing school in 1931. In that year she made her debut at the Grosse Pointe Club as one of the six debutantes who each year were honored at the Big Six Ball held during the holiday season. A betrothal party formally marking the couple's engagement was held in Detroit in November 1937; and in the first week of December Ellen and her parents traveled to Key West for the wedding, which took place on December 11 (O'Grady).

Shortly thereafter the couple moved to La Jolla, California, which remained Latimer's city of residence to the time of his death on June 23, 1983. Although the trek across country to La Jolla reflects the writer's continued preference for tropical living close to the ocean, in other ways the move marked distinct choices in his career. In 1938 the Crime Club would publish the fourth William Crane novel, the novel of Florida setting called *The Dead Don't Care*. But writing in La Jolla the last of the series, *Red Gardenias* (1939), Latimer was becoming interested in other forms of narrative and other venues for his talent. These included experimenting with untried modes of detective fiction and other forms of the novel, and the script writing for movie studios that he began to engage in.

Red Gardenias makes a fitting closure to the history of the detective William Crane, who began his apprenticeship with the depression decade fear of joblessness and failure. Through the test of five performances, the series demonstrates his merit, and in the denouement of *Red Gardenias*

Crane enters the class of wealth and status by accepting the reward of an upper-class marriage with Ann Fortune, blond, fair-skinned niece of Colonel Black, in effect marrying the boss's daughter. No longer will he associate with sleazy mobsters and taxi dancers or face violence and death. He will instead manipulate words and images for the March Corporation to create advertising campaigns promoting domestic products like refrigerators and dishwashers. The decade of austerity ends fittingly with anticipation of a new distribution of wealth in war-time boom and post-war consumerism. Person and persona resolve their lives in parallel histories: Crane's linked rewards of a good marriage, material success, and new career; Latimer's marriage to a Grosse Pointe debutante, royalties from Doubleday and Universal Studios for his detective novels, and the movement into a newer technology for the distribution of commodified language, that is, the film writing that helped facilitate the phenomenal growth of the film industry through the 1930s and into the next decade.

In La Jolla Latimer weighed his prospects judiciously. He remained interested in writing detective fiction, though he found the nature of his interest changing. As the Crime Club editors at Doubleday knew, he had found an audience for comedy with his William Crane. He had emphasized the character's glib, breezy irreverence, his alcoholic antics, bawdy escapades, and eccentric means of resolving cases. Latimer's publisher wanted more of the same in the different package he offered them with the amateur detective Peter Coffin, the new series initiated with *Search for My Great-Uncle's Head*. It would retain the comedic treatment with the introduction of the new protagonist, an intelligent but boyish, untried bumbler of an absent-minded history professor; it would also bring Colonel Black actively into the narrative out of the remoteness of his executive offices.[9]

But Latimer had grown disenchanted with the Peter Coffin character. He had written the novel because he didn't wish to turn out too many William Cranes in quick succession. Despite the publisher's satisfaction with *Great-Uncle's Head*, the writer liked neither the book nor the new character (*Megavore* 17-18). Probably, Latimer felt that the new detective he had chosen was simply another manifestation of the apprentice-at-life character he'd developed in William Crane, and that in his new California existence such a persona could no longer draw power from his own inner experience.

Also at issue were the strictures publishing decorum placed upon language, particularly that dealing with sexual experience, about which much could be implied but little directly presented. In the Crime Club editions of the William Crane novels Latimer had managed to present the personality of his detective without emasculating him, tempering his alcoholic excess, or stripping away the reality of his ethnic and gender prejudices. But he concluded the editing of *The Dead Don't Care* and *Red Gardenias* for *Collier's* feeling that the novels had been compromised (Latimer, "There's..." 372).[10]

Ready for change he therefore turned to the African safari novel *Dark Memory* (1940) and then to his most extreme hard-boiled detective mystery, *Solomon's Vineyard* (1941). It is reasonable to believe that in choosing these new paths he felt insured against the possibility of failure by certain developments: his history of success with Doubleday, which should surely buy good will; his developing career as a film writer, which gave him a cushion of income if his fiction writing failed; and the film industry itself, where he might exploit the market established with the three William Crane books made into movies.

In *Dark Memory* Latimer tested a new narrative model. It is in part a novel about a scientific expedition into the Belgian Congo in search of gorilla specimens; it is also an adventure story about the efforts of a glamorous and distraught wife to recover her missing scientist-explorer husband. Published by Doubleday, the book made too little stir to encourage the writer toward more of its kind; it received mixed reviews, including one devastating response in *The Saturday Review of Literature*.[11] In time Latimer dismissed the novel, begging faulty memory about his reasons for writing it (*Megavore* 19). There seems to be little doubt, however, that he conceived it as grist for the Hollywood mills that had discovered an audience for films about colonial India and Africa and modern safaris into Africa's deep reaches. The publication of *Dark Memory* in April, 1940 occurred within a spread of months from August 1939, through August 1940, during which no fewer than 12 movies of such setting were released by the major studios, with titles like *Green Hell, Congo Maisie, Zanzibar, Safari*; and the vogue for such movies continued into the decade.

But Latimer's true talent as novelist lay in detective fiction, as the uncompromising *Solomon's Vineyard* proves. The novel goes back to a subject he first encountered as a *Herald* and *Trib* reporter in Chicago—the story of the House of David, a religious colony in Benton Harbor,

Michigan. Developing as an expression of millenarian belief, the House of David colony had become a vigorous religious and economic force, its wealth based mostly on the sale of agricultural products and its large amusement park attractive as a summer resort. In Latimer's time the colony was in decline because of fraud and sexual scandal in its leadership and consequent prosecution by state and federal authorities. The novel's detective Karl Craven is hired by an uncle to recover his niece from the colony, where she has been proselytized and held in a brainwashed condition as a sexual slave (and no writer's exaggeration of historical fact regarding certain of the young women of the colony).

Latimer thought of *Solomon's Vineyard* as his most successful novel, the book for which he most wished to be remembered (*Megavore* 19). In the PI Karl Craven, he maintained certain parallels with the marginal William Crane and Peter Coffin characters; all are conscious of the distance between themselves and the patriarchal arbiters of culture and success. Like Crane and Coffin, the alliteratively affinitive Craven has an implicit identification with good class; he has attended Notre Dame and achieved some fame as a football player but failed to complete his degree. Unlike his predecessors, however, he chooses to remain in his marginal condition—an extreme alienation that he finds satisfying as a source of self-authenticity and power. The sado-masochistic sexual relation between Craven and the Princess (the consort of the prophet Solomon who manages the religious colony) is directly represented, as is Craven's sadistic pleasure in the violence he directs toward males who resist him. Fearing a libel suit, Doubleday did not exercise its option to publish the novel. Because Latimer turned to the British house of Metheun for its publication in 1941, the novel remained relatively unknown to his readers until its American publication in 1946, even then appearing in bowdlerized form.

Following this unfortunate history, Latimer ceased for the time being to write detective fiction for book publication and devoted himself to the film writing that had already begun to occupy his interest. In the summer of 1938 the Columbia Pictures producer Joseph Sistrom had made contact with the writer in La Jolla. Sistrom read and was impressed by Latimer's work; and he invited an audition treatment for the mounting of one of the many Lone Wolf films that were a basic commodity at Columbia Pictures. Working from Louis Joseph Vance's *The Lone Wolf's Daughter*, he prepared a script that Sistrom approved, receiving thus his first studio commission. The Columbia Pictures production of *The Lone Wolf Spy Hunt*, with Sistrom as producer and Peter Godfrey as director, was released on January 19, 1939. It was the first of several professional associations with Sistrom, with whom Latimer developed what he considered his deepest Hollywood friendship (*Megavore* 19).[12]

There followed from 1939 to 1942 the commissions to write or co-write scripts of five films for Columbia, M.G.M., United Artists, and Paramount Studios. Collectively, the movies reflect shifting combinations of certain narrative elements that Latimer had manipulated in his fiction writing: a linear adventure plot, the centrality of a male lead, gender and ethnic comedy, with a heavy dose of mystery and puzzle solving. Most of the films are detective adventures, if not in source or name then certainly in effect. All cast in leading roles actors recognized for their masculine appeal, such as Walter Pidgeon, Robert Preston, Brian Donlevy, and Alan Ladd. Of these film scripts probably the most significant was that written for the second version of Dashiell Hammett's *The Glass Key*, released by Paramount on August 28, 1942.

Given this development Latimer might say that while the circumstances of publishing *Solomon's Vineyard* in 1941 proved frustrating, they did not conclude his writing career or his use of the materials of detective fiction, which recycled well in the newer venue. He reaped material benefit from what he called "that lovely script writing money" (*Megavore* 18). In La Jolla the Latimers purchased a house and started the family that would include Ellen Jane, namesake Jonathan, and Nicholas, as well as the appropriate family pets—two Airedales called Bill Crane and Doc Williams after the series characters. From his home the writer commuted by train or air to Los Angeles, where he worked in studio facilities during the most sensitive periods of script preparation. An interview in the December 1941 *Writer* gives an impression of Latimer's satisfaction in that time. Working on the script of *Murder at the Mardi Gras* (renamed *Night in New Orleans*), he received Pauline Gale in his Paramount office and spoke reflectively of theory, technique, and rewards with an enthusiasm that seems genuine and not simply in the service of the gospel of success characteristic of that magazine.

The script for *The Glass Key* was to be, however, the last of his work for the time. The entry of the United States into World War II saw Latimer volunteer for naval service only to be turned down for poor eyesight. Other factors did not make him a strong candidate for service, since at the time of the Pearl Harbor attack he was 35 years of age with a dependent wife and child. Completing a series of eye exercises, however, improved his sight sufficiently to qualify for voluntary service and during the years 1942-1945 Latimer served in the U.S. Navy, mostly as executive officer on a destroyer assigned to convoy duty in the Atlantic and Mediterranean.

Following his discharge from the Navy, he returned to La Jolla and film work in Hollywood. During the period 1946-1958 he wrote or co-wrote, at various intervals of productivity as studios delayed or advanced dates of release, the scripts for fifteen movies. The year 1948 was especially productive, seeing the release of four films on which he worked; but in general he was engaged in one or two films each year. A hiatus of three years occurred from August 1953 to August 1956 when he turned to writing the detective novel *Sinners and Shrouds* (1955) and several television scripts. His postwar film writing was performed for various studios: RKO, Warner Brothers, Universal, a British studio (Romulus), and Paramount. However, in nine films Paramount Studios made the most use of Latimer's writing talent, and he did ten films with the director John Farrow.

Their subjects showed more diversity than in the prewar scripts. Two movies of military subject dealt with postwar complications of battle experience: *Beyond Glory* (1948) and *Submarine Command* (1951). *Botany Bay* (1953) screened an adventure story based upon the colonial history of Australia as presented in the novel by Charles Nordhoff and James Hall. Latimer also scripted two westerns: *Copper Canyon* (1950) and *The Redhead and the Cowboy* (1951).

But in consistency with Latimer's prewar film writing, most of the remainder are variations upon the materials of crime or detective melodrama that Latimer had developed facility and reputation for handling. Indeed, some of those of apparently different subject are detective stories in faint mask, as in the story of the cowboy Gil in *The Redhead and the Cowboy*, who must find a murderer or be condemned as a murderer. Of the crime or detective melodramas, several are significant in the history of *film noir*: *Noctourne* (1946), *Alias Nick Beal* (1949), and the 1948 films based on Kenneth Fearing's *The Big Clock* and Cornell Woolrich's *The Night Has a Thousand Eyes*. For good reason Latimer considered *The Big Clock* adaptation to be the best of his film writing (*Megavore* 19); and the writer's greatest overall contribution to film history in his career from 1939 to 1958 lies in the writing of those movies that belong to the *film noir* tradition.

In two postwar novels Latimer returned to detective fiction: *Sinners and Shrouds* (1955) and *Black Is the Fashion for Dying* (1959). Each novel forges linkage between narrative content and the author, who had altered his private life by divorce and a new marriage to Jo Ann Hanzlik in 1955, and who at middle age looked backward upon a life spent as a writer. Presenting another character whose surname begins with *C* (Crane, Coffin, Craven), in *Sinners* Latimer gives us a Sam Clay who has suffered a nasty divorce and is going through a period of boozing and grief; he has been employed for some years in Chicago as a reporter for a newspaper very like the *Trib*. In *Black* the divorced Richard Blake has made a career of writing films; he is engaged in writing an African safari film under circumstances Latimer knew very well. Although the protagonists of both novels are said to be in their thirties, they seem to possess the world weariness and balance of greater maturity; theirs is a retrospective if not valedictory stance as they look backward over the shoulder into their pasts.

These detective novels of Latimer's maturity are, moreover, markedly different in narrative technique from those of 1935-1941. In the prewar novels the writer's strength lay in the manipulation of conventions shared by reader and writer, in the pleasurable exercise of stereotype. To be sure, they went beyond that toward idiosyncratic meanings produced by Latimer's sense of class structure, the social tensions and political doctrines of the decade and the writer's feel for parodic echoes from the narrative traditions he wrote in. They also possessed troubling implications and psychological depths in the treatment of gender and class of which the writer himself may not have been fully aware. Current reprintings of novels from this earlier period suggest the hold these earlier of Latimer's imaginative landscapes continue to have for readers.[13]

In contrast, the postwar detective fiction *Sinners and Shrouds* offers in the density of detail and reference a more fully realized sense of felt life than in the earlier fiction and in *Black Is the Fashion for Dying* a willingness to make an interesting experiment in the manipulation of shifting narrative point of view. In their movements toward closure, the novels also give us protagonists who develop wisdom about how the institutions they serve—journalism and the film industry—generate evils that taint all whose energies make the institutions work, including the word smiths themselves. Looking backward to find the source of corruption, they find it in their own managers, the newspaper publishers and movie producers whose stock is the version of reality their word-and-image machines make and whose fear of losing control of their institutions promotes inner corruption.[14] For in these latter novels Jonathan Latimer's vision draws him to a final analysis of evil that sees its source not only in the founders but also those who have blindly served and whose accurate reading of the past might have made them truer stewards of its meaning. With their world-weary denial and repudiation, his final narratives temper the naive affirmation with which, in the William Crane series, the cycle of Jonathan Latimer's fiction began.

Notes

[1]This interview will be referred to as *Megavore* throughout the rest of the text.

[2]The writer *had* published the first three of the William Crane novels, though none (not two) was dramatized for stage and three (not two and not the first three) were scripted for movies.

[3]No doubt Ickes was taken with the younger Latimer. A report in the 17 May 1936 *Chicago Tribune* makes the assessment that Ickes' friendship with Latimer's father was decisive in placing the novelist on the Publicity Department payroll. The period of employment in Washington was an episode in the writer's life that he seems largely to have dismissed except for speaking of it with Lew Scarr at the end of his career. His children knew nothing of it. It is never named in the many annual reports of activity the writer filed with the Knox College alumni office. He gives the misleading impression in the Megavore interview with McCahery that when he left the *Chicago Tribune* he moved immediately to Key West. One can only speculate about Latimer's reasons for ignoring his Washington tenure, which his father records. His name does not appear in personnel records of the Department of the Interior or the Public Works Administration in the National Archives nor in the records of employees held in the National Personnel Records Center in St. Louis. The reason may simply be that he was paid out of funds for temporary appointment (as opposed to career positions), and no records of employees under limited contract appear to have been kept.

[4]Ickes defended himself: "I went over that manuscript, spending many days on it, revising, eliminating, adding, and changing. It wasn't my book in the sense that I did all my research work and wrote every word of it myself. It was my book in the sense that the thoughts were mine, the language was mine, and the final form was mine" (*Secret Diary* 668).

20 Stewards of the House

[5]For Key West and Monroe County the Depression had disastrous effects, particularly in 1934 and 1935 because of severe reductions in commercial shipping and the closing of the naval yards, as James McLendon details in *Papa: Hemingway in Key West, revised,* (Key West, FL: Langley Press, 1990) 116-123.

[6]The current appearance of Latimer's Margaret Street residence offers a remarkable index into Key West metamorphoses. Its portico is stuccoed with scintillant rocks and seashells, the yard dominated by a gaudy religious shrine.

[7]Latimer took no part in scripting his William Crane novels for Universal. *Headed for a Hearse* was filmed as *The Westland Case* (review *New York Times* 23 October 1937, 14:2). *Lady in the Morgue* was filmed under the author's title (review *New York Times* 9 May 1938, 13:3). *The Dead Don't Care* became *The Last Warning* (review *New York Times* 8 December 1938, 34:4). The movies served the career of the super masculine Preston Foster and were not reviewed with much enthusiasm. Latimer thought they were all right, given that "all three films were...made as cheaply as possible" (*Megavore* 17).

[8]Gale writes rather breezily: "Ernest Hemingway is a friend of [Latimer's], and their method of writing is similar, in physical aspect." In 1980 Latimer commented to McCahery, "I'm sure I was influenced by Hemingway...whom I admired" (*Megavore* 20).

[9]The editorial publicity blurb especially emphasizes Peter Coffin's eccentricity of means:

The story is so full of unusual twists and episodes that it is impossible to mention them all in a brief space, but among the outstanding are a man who dances barefoot on the lake shore in the moonlight, a murder which involves chloroform, shooting and decapitation, a game known as Dr. Tutmiller's Abdominal Reduction Exercise, Lady Cleo, a very amiable cow, another decapitation, and a man who takes joy in throwing boiled chickens, pies, and loaves of bread into the lake with the exclamation, "There, eat that!"

[10]*The Dead Don't Care* was serialized in Collier's as *A Queen's Ransom,* 4 December 1947 through 5 February 1938. *Red Gardenias* was serialized 10 June 1939 through 5 August 1939. As an interesting index into the 1930's sense of good taste, it was more Crane's licentious and bibulous nature than his ethnic prejudices that were remarked by contemporary reviewers, who of course helped draw the parameters of decency that Latimer worked within. Upon the release in 1957 of *Headed for a Hearse* in the Dell Great Mystery Library, the N.A.A.C.P. objected to Crane's use of the word *nigger*, a word that seems to have been editorially acceptable in 1935. Latimer could only respond by urging the social reality from which the detective was drawn: "I suggested [the N.A.A.C.P.] find Crane and straighten *him* out, but I guess Dell couldn't find him" (*Megavore* 18).

[11]Clinton Wells wrote: "If you like your hero manly, your heroine beautiful and lusty, your villain according to tradition, subsidiary characters interesting, your locale glamorous, and your description vivid and convincing, then plotless *Dark*

Memory will leave pleasant memories." *Saturday Review of Literature* 22 (20 April 1940): 18.

[12]The chronological record of Latimer's film writing appears in the appended bibliography. Information here is drawn from Jay Robert Nash and Stanley Ralph Ross, *The Motion Picture Guide* (Chicago: Cinebooks, 1986) and *Variety Film Reviews 1907-1980* (New York: Garland, 1983). The writer's friendship with movie people appears to have been fairly broad; the Latimers received Hollywood and La Jolla guests frequently. The less sociable Raymond Chandler appealed to Latimer for help in entertaining the visiting novelist J.B. Priestly. Chandler observed that Priestly

> was not entirely satisfied with my company, for which I do not at all blame him, and suggested gently that tonight possibly we might meet some of the fellows. So this morning I burst into tears and threw myself at the feet of Jonathan Latimer, who knows everybody and likes everybody (whereas I am just the opposite), so tonight I am going to take him over to Latimer's house, where will be gathered a reasonable selection of what passes for intelligent humanity in our city.

Chandler to Hamish Hamilton, 14 Feb. 1951, *Selected Letters of Raymond Chandler*, ed. Frank MacShane (New York: Columbia University, 1981) 260.

[13]In 1988 International Polygonics, Ltd. reissued *The Lady in the Morgue* and *Solomon's Vineyard*; in 1989 *Murder in the Madhouse* and *The Search for My Great-Uncle's Head*; in 1990 *Headed for a Hearse*.

[14]During the years 1960-65 Latimer made his final career change to television writing for the Perry Mason series, for which he adapted 50 Erle Stanley Gardner books and wrote 45 original scripts. After 1965 he became semi-retired, dying of lung cancer in La Jolla on June 23, 1983, at age 76.

Chapter 2
William Crane Series:
The Agency Man of the New Deal

i. *Marginal Man Becomes Manager*

The series detective William Crane wisecracked through five assignments from the Colonel Black Detective Agency: *Murder in the Madhouse* (1935), *Headed for a Hearse* (1935), *The Lady in the Morgue* (1936), *The Dead Don't Care* (1938), and *Red Gardenias* (1939). The William Crane novels possess an organic character separating them from the writer's other detective fiction of the same period: the essays into amateur-detective narrative (*The Search for My Great-Uncle's Head*, 1937) and into strictly hard-boiled convention (*Solomon's Vineyard*, 1941).

Helping shape this distinctive series identity is Latimer's vision of urban life in the depression years. The writer's experience during the early 1930s as a newspaper journalist in Chicago promoted the gritty street reality of the novels. They have largely a city setting (Chicago, Miami, and a suburban "Marckton"), a landscape upon which the socially divided struggle for the possession of wealth and power. The rural scene exists only in side glances of apple orchard, dairy farm, and duck waters commodified as bootleg applejack, gangster hideout, and undeveloped oil reserve. In Latimer's city, class distinction defines character and manifests itself through the politics of personality, in the social comedy of an elitism based upon taste and consumption, and by often shockingly abrupt and grotesque acts of violence. The gangsterism which defied Prohibition extends into the decade as a crude fist gloved by only apparently benign social surfaces, introducing the theme of pervasive social corruption central to the series. Above all, dollar consciousness absorbs Latimer's characters, whatever their identity by class. Their fear of life without money, the depression-era prospect of poverty, devastates them. The possession and use of wealth as display and means of pleasure consumes their waking dreams. Some of them will do anything for money, including, of course, murder.

22

With the significant exception of the manufacturing tycoon Simeon March in *Red Gardenias*, the originators of the wealth so fought over and productive of criminal behavior are curiously absent from these narratives. The wealth (almost always a great family fortune) has been gathered in an earlier time by men of business genius who have sealed away inheritances in family trusts or securities for the benefit of wives and protection against misuse by prodigal children, faithless executors, or undeserving hangers-on. From the grave the patriarchs continue to exercise control. With these founders—the dead fathers, and their surviving siblings and widows present to narrative—Latimer seems to associate certain traditional virtues: the conservation of social standards and the philanthropic application of wealth. However stodgy and old-fashioned the surviving founders may seem to the detective, William Crane maintains a certain respect.

As the novels appeared, critics commonly observed their themes of violence, drunkenness, and sensuality, a perspective by which it is clear they thought of Latimer's William Crane as a hard-boiled detective in the convention originated by the *Black Mask* writers and extended by other contemporaries. Although such themes are indeed present, they fail to distinguish the truer essence of Latimer's series fiction, which synthesizes puzzle-mystery and hard-boiled narrative toward the writer's idiosyncratic vision.

Toward this synthesis Latimer represents his William Crane as occupying a special medial position that is in kind like that of the tough-guy private eye. In his *Adventure, Mystery, and Romance* John G. Cawelti defines the hard-boiled detective as "a marginal professional" in rebellion against "ordinary concepts of success and respectability." His profession places him within the lower middle class, but his social perspective is that of a common man (142-143). Such a definition has useful application to Dashiell Hammett's Sam Spade in *The Maltese Falcon* (1930). As a gesture of commonness, Spade recurrently rolls his own cigarettes from Bull Durham rather than use expensive ready-mades, as in the brand consciousness exhibited by Latimer's William Crane, who prefers Lucky Strikes and Camels, Heineken's beer, Dewar's scotch, Brooks Brothers haberdashery, etc. Spade's roll-your-owns is a depression-era image of necessity, the make-do that any Kansas wheat farmer or McKeesport steelworker would have easily recognized. In contrast Crane's upscale choices reflect the yearning to be released from the harshness of economic reality.

Like Spade's, William Crane's marginality gives him richness of perspective, since he stands in detachment between the fundamental divisions of his experience. Even so, William Crane is no proletarian hero. There is ultimately little of the alienation characteristic of Hammett's loners Spade or the Continental Op, but much of the Nick Charles who loves money, woman, and the good life in *The Thin Man* (1933). At age 30, Latimer's Detective William Crane is no longer a youth, but neither has he yet become a successful professional, a husband and father, or the failure he fears becoming. At the opening of his detective career, he demonstrates education but no class advantage, ambition but no performance, taste but no means. Of indistinct class, Crane perceives with amusement the details of social difference. He has no illusions about the affectations of the upper nor the crudity of the lower class. His marginality eases movement between the classes. His ready assimilation to caste provides distinct advantage in detective work, for he can enter the dives and strip joints of the Loop as well as the drawing-rooms and penthouses of the exclusive North Shore suburbs or the near Northside. In his private life he sometimes reveals ambivalence toward class identity, as in his conscious preference for the honest directness and attainability of lower-class women in contrast to the dissimulation and indifference of the upper-class women who inflame his sexual fantasies.

But he finds no validity in separateness, discovers no self-authenticity in alienation, as seems true of many a hard-boiled dick. Without illusions about how shallow life among the wealthy elite may be, he is nonetheless drawn to their standards of success, and especially consumerism as its mark. William Crane desires to be identified as an unacknowledged son of the remote patriarchs and to certify his legitimacy by revealing, through his detective work, his own merit and the deceit and criminality of the pretender sons. For the detective's good work restores and preserves the original wealth placed under threat by prodigal children or false claimants. By this means he hopes to enter the class of his true identity and enjoy the status, display, and pleasures that his rightfully won patrimony affords.

In the Crane series the sign of rightful place is the habitation of the wealthy—the house in its various manifestations as country estate, posh apartment, swank hotel room, Lake Forest mansion, Key Largo palace, and the Marchton designer house the detective finally occupies as his own.

The image of the house locates class structure, as in British puzzle-mystery convention, though Latimer shapes it to the American occasion and his own vision. Crane's ambivalence toward it is recurrent. It is occupied by the wealthy grown decadent, as reflected in their insanity, insularity, and elitism. Still, the detective knows his place; he's a visitor in those upper reaches himself. As an example, in the Chicago of *Lady in the Morgue* it is the businessman's Hotel Sherman for himself and crew but the aristocratic Blackwood's for the Courtland elders, toward whom is expected the hat-in-hands deference Crane offers when he delivers reports. His function as detective is to preserve the patriarchal space against assaults from within and the efforts of the underclass and the criminal class to enter. He becomes, therefore, the steward of the house.

His efforts to become its master as well reflect Latimer's ingenious portraiture of his William Crane and the Colonel Black Detective Agency as a representation of the larger economic model that appeared during the 1930s to be in a state of collapse: the industrial management model by which labor was organized into fruitful work through managers whose intellectual power and force of personality transformed the will and capital of corporate boards and chairmen into useful commodity.

Working for the Black Detective Agency, Latimer's William Crane has the ability to move between the classes of labor and capital and organize the work that completes assignments (the industrial product) given him by Colonel Black. The Colonel receives commissions because the wealthy privately know him as one of their own who can be entrusted with their investment (always a handsomely large amount, with expense accounts William Crane loves to exhaust) to produce the commodity they desire, namely the piece of detection by which the safety of their own wealth is preserved from threat of dissolution. Rarely appearing directly in the narratives (as if from a distant boardroom), by telephone and telegram Colonel Black places directives with his manager Crane in the interior cities of Chicago, Miami, or Marchton, where the manufacture of the product occurs.

In those urban spaces through five novels William Crane perseveres in a continuing state of apprenticeship. Despite his comic bawdiness, alcoholic excess, and eccentric technique, he views his work as a test, recurrently feeling anxiety about Colonel Black's satisfaction with his job performance. To enter the class of the wealthy he must receive the approval of its patriarchs by displaying the behaviors that testify to his true birth; and the last of the series novels, *Red Gardenias*, shows us his success in carrying off yet another work assignment and receiving the ultimate rewards: an upscale marriage with Colonel Black's modish blonde niece, Ann Fortune (thing and word in happy juncture), and entry into the higher estate as an advertising executive for the March Corporation. Latimer's William Crane has found his place in anticipation of a consumer paradise, post-Depression America.

ii. *Murder in the Madhouse (1935)*

The first series novel, *Murder in the Madhouse*, takes place in a private sanitarium close to "Toryville." (Clearly, Latimer has in mind Tarrytown, New York, and the Hudson Valley region.) There Dr. Livermore has assembled a staff of doctors, nurses, and ward attendants to provide psychiatric and medical services for the wealthy insane. Commissioned by the brother of the patient Miss Van Kamp, Colonel Black has assigned William Crane to enter the sanitarium disguised as a madman to determine if Miss Van Kamp's fears for her safety have any basis in fact. From her have been stolen a box containing $400,000 and one of two keys to a bank vault in New York containing another $800,000 worth of cash, jewelry, and bonds. The secret efforts of Drs. Livermore and Eastman and the aide Charles (each in shifting conspiratorial affiliations with Nurse Evans) to steal the box and key set in motion the several murders of the novel, their resolution, and the recovery of Miss Van Kamp's wealth.

In various ways the novel reflects Latimer's indebtedness to puzzle-mystery convention. The remote estate-like sanitarium gathers into a contained private space these members of the upper class (the patients) with their servants (the staff) and becomes a microcosm of history and social organization. In his disguise as a patient, his glibness of speech and easy savoir, his fastidiousness of dress and fondness for Harris tweed, William Crane has putative identification with the class he serves. The detective's confidant of ordinary intelligence appears in Doc Williams, who enters the sanitarium in the disguise of a worker come to repair a short circuit caused by Crane. The duel of wit and ratiocinative ability in the first interview between Crane and Dr. Livermore establishes the detective's superior mind. His explanations to Sheriff Walters about the differences between simple and advanced deduction, the several allusions to Poe's original detective C. Auguste Dupin, the murders offstage, the display to the reader of all the clues, the retirement into thought by the detective, the formal denouement that logically reduces mystery and charges the true murderers (Charles and Nurse Evans) before the gathered survivors, all these clearly establish Latimer's indebtedness to the lineage of Edgar Allan Poe and Arthur Conan Doyle.[1]

The narrative, however, moves beyond naive imitativeness toward a formal self-consciousness of special service to the writer's vision. Latimer's series detective is not simply a mirror image of the bloodless gentleman protagonist, a sort of parallel to S. S. Van Dine's Philo Vance of affected speech and manner. Against certain expectations of action, class, and status implicit in the form, Latimer places his own campy sensibility, his own native feel for American time and space. (Surely Latimer intends the several parodic echoes here, as for example his reversal of the convention of the closed room murder by giving us not the victim but the murderer Charles imprisoned inside the securely locked detention room in which he nonetheless manages one last murder!).

Perhaps that is why not its conventionality but its novelty, especially the shocking personal style of Latimer's detective, caught the attention of reviewers. One noted William Crane's "spirituous consumption and his use of slang." Another classified the novel as hard-boiled fiction, observed that indecent language and drinking recur, and added that the characters' "morals are, to put it mildly, not above reproach." Echoing these remarks, yet another reviewer gave his analysis a more telling point by describing Latimer's first novel as "A boyish American-style book without pretension."[2]

In its signs William Crane's world exists in a system of contraries (often dramatic ironies productive of the comedy in the novel), and the detective works his way through a maze of apparent abstract opposites (kindness-cruelty, sanity-insanity, intelligence-stupidity, orthodoxy-fanaticism) as well as real oppositions of class, wealth, and gender. The people Crane encounters are disunities of appearance and reality because of the masks they sanely and insanely affect. They puzzle, amuse, or disgust him since normal expectations of what may be true (doctors and nurses who heal, mental patients driven by compulsion, aides who nurture, etc.) only sometimes correspond with reality. An important disunity of appearance and reality in the novel is the opposition of child and adult behavior. Some characters in the novel possess unreconciled elements of child and adult; they behave like boyish males or adults who regress to childishness (loudness, vulgarity of language, fits of anger, uncensored pleasure seeking, sexual curiosity, etc.).

Among the contrarities of the novel is of course the opposition of sanity-insanity and the continuing play upon meaning produced by uncertainty of limit and definition. In their first meeting Dr. Livermore assures William Crane that insanity has no clear definition, that people simply suffer "from brief periods when their rationality is in abeyance. It is like a nightmare, only it occurs during waking hours" (Latimer, *Murder* 21).[3] In his new identity as a patient, Crane has already experienced waking hours strangely distorted. Looking out the back of the wildly careening ambulance by which he is taken to the sanitarium, he has a sense of the Hudson Valley landscape as an unreal movie panorama, as if "it were being unwound too quickly on a stage set built to represent scenery passing a train window" (3). The motif of life-as-cinema extends from his first view of the sanitarium and grounds which look "as artificial as the setting in a Cecil B. DeMille society drama," to sunlight in trees flickering in erratic movement like that recorded in "early motion-picture films," to Nurse Evans (of no beatific vision, she) as looking like "a scornful Max Reinhardt saint" (13, 101, 270).

From the first, Crane has novel experience that gives him insight into the life of Miss Van Kamp and the other patients, the discovery of how powerless and anonymous the institutionalized have become. He has been cuffed and locked inside an ambulance driven ever more drunkenly by a newly employed aide, Joe Kassuccio, who normally works as an enforcer for a New York bootlegger. As they buy gas and a renewed supply of applejack, the station attendant, startled, observes that Crane is a third passenger. Kassuccio responds: "Oh, he don't count. He's a daffy" (6). It is a point of view lying beneath the patronizing acts of the clinicians William Crane meets and the threats and real violence by which he and the patients are controlled.

And Latimer's narrative continues to play ironically with the indefiniteness of boundaries. Who in this asylum are the crazies, the keepers or the kept? Upon arrival Crane is met by Andrew the security guard, whose religious obsession leads him to believe that God has assigned him the prophetic role of ferreting out sexual depravity inside the institution. With Andrew, the writer can't resist farce or even an old joke; to the detective's question which of them is crazy, the gatekeeper responds: "You are. I'm a guard" (192-94, 39).

Among the kept, Crane observes a range of mental state. Whatever their former illnesses, those of Miss Van Kamp and her companion Miss Paxton seem in total remission. Mr. Richardson exhibits only ordinary jealousy when Mrs. Patterson Heyworth shows interest in the attractive William Crane. Mr. Blackwood and the aging actress Miss Queen suffer fearful anxiety, which nonetheless has basis in the reality that someone is murdering patients. Others are delusory or act out compulsions: Mr. Pittsfield impersonates President Lincoln, Mr. Penny won't talk, Mrs. Brady removes clothing under stress, Mrs. Heyworth searches for her dead husband among the men she meets. Only Mr. L'Adam, with his lycanthropy, seems always to be in the frenzy of his derangement and shows capacity for direct violence. Keeper or kept, all quite reasonably fear him.

Aside from their individual mental condition, the patients' private histories generate a collective impression of a social order whose elite have failed it, of manufacturer, lawyer, investor, stage actress, and society matrons who have lost the ability to organize and control because of broken connections between past and present. There are hints of this in Pittsfield's delusion of grandeur, in his playing Lincoln not as the Great Emancipator but as an organizer of dinner parties, in Mrs. Brady's self-indulgent sentimentality about her lost social advantage, in the wild eyes of Mrs. Heyworth, whose face otherwise shows "skin firm and smooth and soft over delicate bones," a look "patrician" like those "of society girls at Palm Beach and Bermuda" (106).

But the strength lost by this class seems found in Miss Van Kamp, in whom the past somehow remains whole and uncorrupted. In William Crane's first view of her seated in the garden, she seems to be an eternal principle and the true lady of the manor: "There was no wind for a moment and there was a timelessness about the old lady and the garden and the lack of movement, as though she would always be there, motionless and grim and implacable" (34). Persuaded of the new patient's true identity, Miss Van Kamp gives the detective information about the lost valuables box. Without humor they trade the words of the joke that has passed earlier between Crane and the fanatic gatekeeper Andrew: who in the asylum is insane? Miss Van Kamp certainly seems to be in fullest possession of herself. When the detective examines her room, his eyes record the evidence of the stable past and class status Miss Van Kamp seems to represent: an antique patchwork quilt with the date 1812 sewed into it, her attendance at Vassar, a savings deposit book with a large balance, a collection of mementos including a first prize for Sunday school attendance, and among her clothing fine knits and decent respectable woolens (72). She adamantly asserts that her valuables are lost, despite the clinicians' patronizing statements that her wealth is a delusion, that her box of securities contains only scrap paper.

Among the keepers, Crane encounters authority bolstered by a sort of bold condescension, or outright threat and violence. Not all the clinicians—Dr. Buelow and Nurse Clayton are notable exceptions—have private agendas, but Crane feels manipulated by the sanitarium environment. On the first evening, he attends what the patients call "movies," a filmed light show of shifting colors, music, and scents produced by machine, all designed to relax them before bedtime. The light show offers yet another instance of the motif of life-as-cinema, and Crane receives the impression of psychiatric quackery.

For good reason the detective feels distrustful, not just because he has encountered among the keepers the guard Andrew's blatant madness but because he has experience of the more subtle fear, greed, and anger contained within the personality of the keepers which propel their violence. For the keepers contain madness also. Ostensibly, Dr. Livermore has hired Joe Kassuccio as a new hospital aide, but he in fact serves as a bodyguard since secretly the doctor fears his colleague Dr. Eastman. When the ride-cramped Crane has difficulty standing, the hired muscle pulls him from the ambulance onto gravel, giving him bloody abrasions. Inside the sanitarium the hoodlum bangs Crane's head against a wall. His violence seems contagious. While the detective's personal history is taken by Dr. Livermore, the wolf man L'Adam escapes from detention; and Crane observes the psychiatrist arm himself with pistol, chain, and baseball catcher's mask as a means of recapturing the deranged man (16-17, 24).

Violence between keeper and kept continues. Crane suffers a night assault from unknown attackers (as he discovers, Dr. Eastman and Nurse Evans) by whom he is once more beaten. Deciding that the patient Blackwood is the probable murderer, Dr. Eastman directs the aides to beat and terrorize the innocent man into confession (90-91, 112-13). The detective responds to such violence in kind. At the end of his entry interview (Crane has already been assaulted in the ambulance and hallway), Dr. Livermore threatens him; and the detective gets in good hits upon Joe and the ambulance driver, as well as kicks to the stomach and jaw of Dr. Eastman (31).

Despite its recurrence, Latimer's representation of violence in *Murder in the Madhouse* does not dwell upon the sadistic pleasures of pain (McCahery)⁴. The single exception is Crane's assault upon Joe Kassuccio, whom the detective waylays in a sudden fierce attack:

Mr. Kassuccio grunted and fell on his back, his head a dark blob on the white pebbles in the path. Crane put his right heel in the exact center of the upturned face and threw his entire weight onto his right leg. Then he spun clockwise. There was a cracking sound, and under his heel it felt juicy. He stepped off the face, rubbed his heel on the grass at the side of the walk, and then walked swiftly to the guest house. (197)

Although Latimer's detective here clearly enjoys a gratuitous pleasure beyond utility, the instance is not characteristic. The violence of the novel occurs in contexts of humor and irony that soften it. However immoderate Dr. Livermore's pursuit of the wolf man with pistol and chain may seem, the incongruity of his wearing a baseball catcher's mask gives the scene the character of farce. Crane's bruises damage his good looks and make his body ache. Really, he'd rather not be doing all this hitting but wryly gives and accepts his blows as if the violence were contained in the rules of the detective game, another male sport. Often Crane gets and gives his licks in a comedy of violence by which the hurts seem painful pratfalls. Already the object of two assaults, in the presence of Dr. Livermore he enters the first fight with the hired muscle Joe and the chauffeur under the vain hope his disguise as wealthy deranged patient will give him some immunity. (It doesn't.) As they force him to his room, he calls out wildly: "You can't lock me up....I am C. Auguste Dupin." Struck to the ground in a night assault, he seizes the leg of one attacker and becomes aware of the irony of sheer silk hose and a very sharp high heel planted on his wrist. His own greatest violence, the attack upon Dr. Livermore's thug, is motivated by the desire for retribution; for if revenge justifies violence, Crane's attack upon Joe Kassuccio certainly bears that sanction.

As participant in violence William Crane's attitude seems like that of the brash child who twits adults and asserts himself through playful gestures veiling the ambivalence of fight-flight ("I was only playing," when the game grows too rough). This aspect of personality, the child who is in the man, seems central to Latimer's representation of the detective. It expands to include certain cathexes of emotional energy: authority, sexuality, work.

Having accepted his new persona, Crane discovers that he has regressed from his status as an autonomous, working adult male to that of child-like dependency and restriction. His first impression of Dr. Livermore is four-fold: The man has the appearance of success (a large diamond ring), he looks patriarchal (largeness of size, a black beard), he has secret intimacy with a female (face powder on his coat), and his eyes are "cunning and indirect" (18). (With the image of the great black beard of Dr. Livermore, Crane associates two heroic, senior males of 30's renown, Gen. Italo Balbo and Sir Hubert Wilkins.[5]) In his care Dr. Livermore's patients exist in the condition of children who fear the means of his authority (the loss of privilege, the warm baths to calm them, the assignment to detention rooms if disobedient). Like children they flee in self-isolation to their rooms or curry favor by careful observance of his regimen. Crane is forbidden liquor and indirectly denied association with women. The prohibitions of the censorious, denying father extend to the staff, who engage in furtive drinking or sexual intimacy (Nurse Twilliger with Joe in the garage, Crane with Nurse Evans in the garage, Nurse Evans with the aide Charles in her room, Nurse Evans with Dr. Eastman, indeed, Nurse Evans with the old reprobate Dr. Livermore himself, who can't repress his own libido any more than his children!).

Carrying out his truth-seeking adult work as a detective, Crane uses an adolescent verbal pattern—wisecracking—to challenge the authority of the patriarchal psychiatrist and his control over patients and staff. In their first interview the boy-detective agrees to cooperate docilely with the father-psychiatrist. Yet his eyes record the evidence of the doctor's secret erotic life with Nurse Evans while he wisecracks irreverently to the obvious irritation of the clinician and the pleasure of Nurse Clayton. A recurrent mode of his speech in the series novels, the detective's aggressive wisecracking is the linguistic equivalent to physical horseplay. Both express the ambivalence of fight-flight. Like horseplay, wisecracking empowers a mild, socialized form of assault. Handled correctly, it's never a losing game. The speaker wins if he's clever enough and doesn't take it too far; but even if he takes it too far and the object loses control in a display of angry reprisal, the wiseguy has shown more restraint and therefore wins. Here Crane as smart-ass son tests the father-doctor's self-control but pushes the elder's contained anger to its discharge in the violent recovery of the wolf man L'Adam and the physical restraint ordered by Dr. Livermore, which is appropriate in kind: the boy-detective is sent to his own room.

Crane's adult work as detective is of course served by his joking by-play. Though everyone considers it an eccentricity of his delusion, it makes a perfectly good cover story to tell Drs. Livermore and Eastman and anybody who asks that he is actually a famous detective (whatever the degree of adolescent boast the "famous" may carry, since he is not yet famous). His joking, deranged manner serves the purpose of gathering information indirectly; and as the kind of puzzle-mystery protagonist his creator Jonathan Latimer has in mind, the wisecracking of this American kid establishes his intellectual superiority.[6] Such an end is served, once more, in the complex opening interview, where what has been a radio-comedy dialogue in which Dr. Livermore is the butt of Crane's smart-guy cleverness turns into a display of ratiocinative ability by which the detective reveals publicly to those assembled that the psychiatrist and Nurse Evans have just been engaged in an erotic interlude. Jealous, Dr. Eastman calls his superior a "son of a bitch," and secret relationships as well as Dr. Livermore's anger are pushed further toward revelation and catharsis (21-23, 28-31).

With women Crane's wisecracking becomes flirtatiousness. As strategy it reflects the detective's recurrent desire-fear ambivalence throughout the series as he comes into contact with alternative pairings of light and dark women who embody varying class and ethnic contrasts such as elitism versus plebianism and Anglo versus Mediterranean cultures. In *Murder in the Madhouse* these are blonde Nurse Evans and brunette Nurse Clayton, with whom as nurses Latimer also associates their common stereotype in male fantasy as lustful sexual beings. Nurse Twilliger displays a decorous public manner, yet owns the primary sexual features of bust and buttocks (she has an S-shaped body) that tell of her "real" nature and drive men to possess her. Nurse Evans, a sort of blonde starlet, magnetizes male libido. In contrast the brunette Nurse Clayton is an attractive pleasant girl, willing to flirt, but in her stable niceness neither victim (like poor funny Twilliger incapable of repressing her itch) nor victimizer (like the ambitious Evans).

With the light-dark women William Crane's flirtatious wisecracking offers a means of control, as for example (once more) in the complexly

significant opening interview between himself and Dr. Livermore. There
he manages to train Nurse Clayton's attention toward himself as individual
rather than patient and lead her away from her professional identity and
the psychiatrist's control over her. In a personal way she thinks he's cute
and funny. Dr. Livermore doesn't, and of course that disaffection is the
product of Crane's wisecracking as a social strategy.

But beneath his flirting, Crane contains fear. It is sex comedy—fun
in the madhouse—when the wild-eyed but otherwise attractive Mrs.
Heyworth enters his room and with no words at all (let alone wisecracks)
becomes the sexual aggressor. From his bed Crane flees in a painful
escape:

He heard himself scream twice, and then he climbed through the open window and
jumped. Bushes broke his fall and scratched his face and shoulders....He raced
through the garden and over to the high wall....Glass and barbed wire along the top
of the wall tore his fingers, and he finally dropped back into the garden. (240)

Crane's sexual ambivalence seems more largely shared by the other
male characters in their reaction to Mrs. Brady's episode of emotional
collapse. Believing that she is next to be killed, the patient gives way to
her compulsion (disrobing) and appears ready to commit suicide by
leaping from the window ledge of her room. It is another scene of sexual
comedy for which this time there exists a large audience—including by
now the sheriff and his deputies, who are, significantly, his sons. Standing
by to rescue the deluded woman, they feel obliged as responsible males
and professionals to preserve the female. Her removal of clothing gestures
her worst fears, yet to the male audience her acts are perceived as a
striptease, and nobody quite sees her *because* of her nakedness.
Confronted with Mrs. Brady's female nudity, the men are preoccupied by
the icon of her body, which is either an obscenity they wish recovered (in
both senses) or a signal to their libido. The sheriff invokes pity by
characterizing her as senescent, placing her in the same sexless category as
the aged and spinsterish Miss Van Kamp ("She's just a harmless old
lady."). But his son Cliff responds: "She's not so old...I got eyes."
Returned to her room, Mrs. Brady barricades herself against the men.
Sheriff Walters refuses to go inside because he is "a married man." The
deputies speak of the difficulty of seizing her, associating her nudity with
common images of female ugliness or danger: "greased pig," "greased

tiger" (159-63).

Her rescue by Dr. Buelow displays his practical wisdom and kindness but proceeds as an implicit seduction. (It also gives Latimer an opportunity to make use of his beloved popular music and jazz.) Knowing Mrs. Brady's longing for the security of her past (including the pleasure of dancing), the psychiatrist plays a recording of "St. Louis Blues," to which he and his patient dance until she is calmed and he can maneuver her to a therapeutic bath. But the dancing is performed to the sensual words and music of the blues song; and Latimer records its vernacular lyrics, which speak with innuendo of sexual yearning and pleasure (164-167). After her treatment (seduction) has calmed (satisfied) her, Mrs. Brady reappears clothed and wearing a woman's facial disguise—her newly reapplied cosmetic mask of powder, mascara, and lipstick—with only the eyes reflecting her true fear (202). Naked or clothed, she seems to the men unknowable except through the doctrine of appearance by which they control their reaction.

And in any event, Mrs. Heyworth and Mrs. Brady exist among the kept as insane women, a category that confers special immunity and an identity not to be confused with other women. Latimer's detective has moral qualms about the sexual exploitation of Mrs. Heyworth, whose derangement it is that compels her to his bed. Even so, it is only in a lesser degree of reaction that he displays the same desire-fear ambivalence toward other women, such as the sane Miss Evans.

As detective, William Crane grows quickly aware that among the keepers she deserves special observation. He hears the ambulance driver's and Joe Kassuccio's lascivious descriptions of the nurse. He himself analogizes her to alternative cinematic images as Sadie Thompson or Max Reinhardt saint. Though she has engaged herself to Dr. Eastman by giving him her sorority pin, she leaves blonde hair on the disarranged cushions of Dr. Livermore's couch and face powder on his coat. Her sensuality draws male energy toward aggression; and when Crane approaches Nurse Evans, he does so in guarded ways, by detached observation or as clowning wise guy.

As observer, he has a voyeur's interest in her. Under the sheriff's detention (having become the murder suspect), he slips out of his room past a drunken guard to the darkness of the garden in order to peep through the windows at Dr. Livermore's activities. In this first instance of his panty fetish, his prurience is excited by seeing Miss Evans in a ti?

silk dress that leaves him to wonder if she wears underclothing. In the series novels William Crane is preoccupied by that issue; and about women who arouse such speculation he feels personal desire and fear beyond that of utility to his function as detective. (In contrast the unthreatening spinster Miss Van Kamp owns the decent woolen underwear of senescence.) Because he is himself drawn to highly eroticized females, he senses the power of such women as Nurse Evans to use the promise of sexual accessibility as a means of organizing events. Such characters affiliate with males of power and authority, but the exact nature of the affiliation often remains uncertain. In this instance Crane seems to have the curiosity of a child who has blundered upon an adult primal scene. As he watches the nurse renew her lipstick, he views her face as archetypically female, possessing a dualism "cold and reserved" but alternatively "quite wanton." Dr. Livermore enters the room in a robe, his hair and beard disordered, his lips "a smeary red." Miss Evans praises his sexual performance, observing that in his desire for pleasure the doctor seems like males generally. The detective hears of the woman's refusal to marry the clinician, the doctor's desperate need to divert Miss Van Kamp's wealth toward running the sanitarium, Nurse Evan's desire for money and an affluent life, and her suggestion that the doctor might hasten the natural end of Miss Van Kamp's life (177-81).

But Crane isn't through gawking and eavesdropping. When Nurse Evans leaves Dr. Livermore and enters Dr. Eastman's rooms he follows the lighted windows to peep further and overhears Dr. Eastman's jealous questions and the woman's protestations of innocence. Crane now understands that Miss Van Kamp's box, first stolen by Dr. Livermore and Nurse Evans, is now thrice stolen, having slipped out of the hands of Dr. Eastman and Nurse Evans into unknown possession. Eastman accuses the woman, who affects hurt feelings and placates her lover in a beguiling way (181-86).

When the nurse leaves Dr. Eastman's rooms to enter the staff building, the voyeur-detective changes his strategy and becomes a flirtatious male on the make. Each knows the game well. He plays at tough-guy by growling a funny threat: "I've got you covered, babe...." She responds in kind: "I'd rather you'd ask for a date next time." When he accuses her of taking part in an attack upon himself, she neither denies nor admits touching her ankle and high heel (the instrument of the attack). He outlines what he has just overheard in her discussion with Dr.

Eastman about Miss Van Kamp's missing box, Miss Evans accuses him of being "just a Peeping Tom," though the detective states his preference for being known as "Watchful William" (186-89).

For the time being, Nurse Evans *becomes* his "date" in the privacy of the garaged ambulance, where she agrees to drink with him and compliantly responds to his questions: ("I could go for an intelligent man," she prompts.) He hears her rationalization of helping Dr. Eastman steal the box from Dr. Livermore as an act of love and her denial of knowing who now has the box or who killed Mr. Pittsfield or Miss Paxton. The scene's subtext of mutual benefit and seduction receives special emphasis when the religious fanatic Andrew, who is always on the watch to ferret out and condemn secret sin, catches them in their hidden liaison. Far gone with illegal applejack and Miss Evans' charms, Crane placates the old man by persuading him that he is the Archangel Gabriel and she, the Virgin Mary. After the gatekeeper leaves, the scene concludes on a note of mutual understanding and the prospect of sexual intimacy (189-197).

As he pushes the narrative toward denouement, Latimer develops an apparent conflict in William Crane's attraction to the woman and his desire to do the job well. Nurse Evans seems a trophy female to the two psychiatrists who seek to hold her by their wealth, power, or seniority. If Crane is a usurping son who challenges Dr. Livermore's patriarchal control of the nurse, the garage scene between the detective and Miss Evans assumes added significance. As physical space remote from the house, garages have a way of offering children a space for experimentation free from adult intrusion. Other furtive liaisons between Nurse Twilliger and Joe occur in this garage. Even Andrew's fanatic, wrathful condemnation of the intimacy between Crane and the blonde nurse seems simply another variation on the theme, a crazy-comics paraphrase of the control of the fathers over the sexuality of their sons.

But in *Murder in the Madhouse* Crane's conflict between love and duty is not persuasively represented. For him the choice is never convincingly that of rebelling against the father-doctor by seducing his woman but rather that of pleasing the absent father-mentor by repudiating the seductress and carrying out the assigned work to the satisfaction of the off-stage Colonel Black. The detective's outer voice of rational plan and the inner voice of lust both say, Follow the Blonde; and the trail of clues leads him finally to the male of deepest secret association, the aide Charles. The reader may feel led on by the least likely, given the woman's preference for virility *and* status and wealth. Still, it's all there. The writer hasn't violated the rules of gamesmanship between himself and reader by withholding clues, although Miss Evans' dedication to the doctrine of romantic love may be a rather late-breaking element of her character in the convoluted story of her assistance in the murder of poor Mr. Penny, who has perceived before the detective has the nurse's true identity as faithful lover of the aide.

In pairing Charles and William Crane as antagonist and protagonist, Latimer followed the puzzle-mystery tradition by which criminal and detective are often seen as mirror images of each other in basic ways: common brilliance, appetites, depravities. A brotherhood exists between these two. They bond in their common violation of the sanitarium rules by drinking in friendship as equals. Seemingly truthful when questioned, the aide never denies being what Crane first perceived him to be: an ex-con who's paid his debt and begs only for the freedom to build a new life by performing well in a job he feels lucky to have.

The basis of his appeal William Crane understands very well. Times are hard; jobs are difficult to find. When the detective becomes angry with Colonel Black for placing him under special peril, his fellow worker Doc Williams observes that the Colonel can always hire someone else to take his place. There are plenty of the jobless. Fearing the loss of employment, Crane responds hastily: "I can take it." In the end Colonel Black never appears to give him a well done, nor does Miss Van Kamp ever thank him for recovering her box from the garden fountain where Charles hid it. Summing up the case, the detective remarks nonetheless his self-satisfaction: "[Miss Van Kamp] wanted her securities back, and I got them for her" (259, 299). The demonstration to Colonel Black is enough; the performance is the reward.[7]

iii. *Headed for a Hearse (1935)*

In the second of the William Crane novels, Jonathan Latimer's native Chicago becomes a symbolic urban space. It is the city as the writer perceived it in his work for the *Herald-Examiner* and *Tribune*—a crude, dynamic arena for the rise and fall of wealth and reputation. Analyses of 1930s Chicago made by other Hearst journalists additionally testify to the vulgar energy that characterized its political and business life.[8] *Headed for a Hearse* shifts in rapid movements between the extremities of Chicago squalor and wealth: from the ugliness of the city jail, the sleazy streets of the south Loop, and the filth of the Chicago River to the interiors of expensive hotels and shops on Michigan Avenue, smart apartments in the near Northside, a brassy wood-paneled brokerage office, and the plush drawing room of a Lake Forest estate (Latimer, *Murder*).[9] Connection seems implicit in the sharp contrasts the detective and his sidekick encounter simply by walking outside a hotel lobby or riding in a taxi: squalor and wealth coexist as discrete but organic elements, functions of a joint process.

The novel shares certain narrative elements with *Murder in the Madhouse*. The wealthy broker Mr. Westland has retained the Colonel Black Detective Agency to represent his interests. To his aid the Colonel sends his employees William Crane and Doc Williams. They are the detective-confidant pair in the puzzle-mystery pattern (including the locked room murder of Mrs. Westland) on which Latimer fleshes out this American novel of Chicago life. The problem of the control of wealth within the upper class generates the major conflict. Detective Crane becomes the object of violence serving a secret conspiracy. Light and dark women become the possible hubs of a dark plot. In order to discover the Truth, once more Crane follows the light woman (here not blonde, but a close-enough redhead) to her true affiliation with the male of agency, one of Westland's own brokerage associates; and once more he boozes and wisecracks a charmed safe path through the black maze of threat, fight, and murder.

But *Headed for a Hearse* also possesses the character of a thriller. Borrowing a common narrative frame from crime fiction, Latimer opens and closes the novel on death row in the Chicago city jail. There the broker Robert Westland awaits execution with the Irish Catholic Dave Connors and the Polish Jew Isadora Verecha. Within a week's time all are to be electrocuted for their crimes. Judged guilty of the murder of his wife, from whom he was estranged, Westland found the trial and the evidence so overwhelming that he fatalistically accepted the sentence. The labor racketeer Connors jars him from apathy and recommends the help of the Jewish criminal lawyer Charles Finkelstein, who in turn contacts Colonel Black. From New York William Crane flies to Chicago and engages in a frantic six-day race against the rushing judgment that takes Connors and Varecha but not his client in the final scene of execution.

From this framework the narrative expands outward toward the representation of Chicago as a vicious sort of Land of Conspicuous

Consumption where dreams of satiation are fulfilled for those who have the money or where those without means are condemned to hungry tantalizing views of the remote bread pudding. William Crane catalogues the show of wealth in the apartment where Mrs. Westland was murdered, its rooms decorated in the best canons of taste, its kitchen fitted with a wine cellar Mr. Westland had custom built in order to keep his expensive collection of wines at correct temperature and humidity (101, 108). Separated from his wife in expectation of their divorce and remarriage with Emily Lou Martin, he has kept one of the two apartment keys for access to the wine, a choice which constituted an element of the evidence against him in his trial.

For the underclass in *Headed for a Hearse*, the experience of wealth comes through vicarious association, petty chiseling, or the sale of illegal services. With William Crane on this high society case, his inferior Doc Williams gawks at the sexy, expensively clothed Emily Lou Martin and Margot Brentino. They are as unattainable as Richard Bolston's "huge tan convertible touring car" which Doc has awed knowledge of as "an English Bentley with a Rolls-Royce body...the fastest semi-stock car in the world. I seen one like it on Long Island last month" (54). The apartment manager knows how to chisel advantage when he rents out the murdered wife's apartment (which in fact is owned by the Westlands) to the dancer Miss Hogan (l06-l07). Miss Hogan, in turn, chooses a sexual liaison with the lawyer Finklestein over William Crane because the lawyer has the persuasive flash of money while the detective has little promise beyond a flirtatious manner (114-15). Chicago City Jail Warden Buckholtz shows a practiced absence of qualms when he accepts the bribe of ten thousand dollars from Mr. Westland to make visits possible with Crane, Finklestein, and other associates as part of their effort to find the true murderer (20).

In his marginality, and a cut above these representatives of the underclass by virtue of his greater intelligence, leadership, and good taste, detective Crane is also powerfully affected by the show-and-tell of money. As manager he has been given a large expense account, which he means to exhaust in food, drink, and entertainment at the kitsch Cafe Monmarte (sic) and the delights of ethnic Italian food at Joe Petro's Restaurant (55-61). Of the underclass that knows the value of dollars and fears bosses, Doc Williams worries about their excessive expenditures upon cab fares and wails and groans when Crane pays a diver five hundred dollars to recover the Webley pistol Richard Bolston has thrown into the Chicago

River (252). Crane possesses, however, the managerial boldness in the use of money necessary to carry out the work given him. Latimer offers an inside joke, considering the writer's then-current association with Harold Ickes in the ghostwriting of the W.P.A. publicity document *Back to Work*, when Crane justifies the distribution of money for such managerial subcontracting by observing: "We're putting more men to work than Roosevelt's recovery program" (241).

But for more private ends Crane also loves the uses of cash. He is greedy for the lifestyle of the leisure class, which he wishes to enter by emulating its forms and activities. With regard to work, he hopes to perform without the appearance of effort toward pecuniary reward, what Thorstein Veblen in *The Theory of the Leisure Class* characterized as "industrial exemption," that is, activity that offers public, symbolic definition of release from productive labor. Though his end is in fact useful product (unlike the leisure class), he wishes to make the work of detecting seem a game of leisure, in the way Westland plays squash at his club or his cousin Lawrence Wharton keeps riding horses. Thus Crane's recurrent boozing, sleeping, and night clubbing that appear to take up so much of his time and energy in pleasure his inferior Doc Williams and (in the later novels) Tom O'Malley are amazed that he is actually able to solve cases. Crane's emulation of the clothing tastes exhibited by the Chicago wealthy also has its source in the economist Veblen's classic analysis that the American leisured wealthy themselves found models of imitation in the forms of aristocratic British life (Veblen 144, 212).

Crane has already been exposed to English models. His boss Colonel Black is a dilettante-scholar of Elizabethan literature who affects tweeds and pipes, and who in this novel is not available to the detective because he is abroad cultivating his interests. The broker Westland meets with his business associates, the detectives, and his lawyer in Warden Buckholtz's office, where they organize their activity in behalf of the condemned man. There Bolston wears a "brown Harris tweed suit fitted smoothly across his broad shoulders, and an Irish linen handkerchief with a brown edge peeked negligently out of his breast pocket." Crane mirrors Bolston, but without the same grace; he is "a tanned, youthful man, and he wore a brown tweed suit like Bolston's, but his was lighter and looked as though he had slept in it" (41, 42). Of the group the most extreme Anglophile is Lawrence Wharton, who belongs to the horsy Lake Forest crowd, wears wool plus fours loose in the English style, keeps a Scotch terrier, affects a toney class accent, and drinks (too much) Scotch whiskey.

Crane is not made bereft of good judgment by what he sees. In their attention to the forms, these Chicago elite can show cloddish if not vicious behavior. Cousin Lawrence doesn't wish to help Westland because Sherlocking is demeaning work, definitely an underclass activity. When Crane and Williams taxi to Lake Forest to consider the details of Wharton's alibi, they interview him, then the alcoholic Amy Dunmar, an elderly wealthy widow who though she could alibi Wharton won't violate her sense of propriety by admitting that she let him spend the night with her on the date in question. Uncertain where detectives belong in the class structure, she doesn't know if she should offer them hospitality; then, offended by their questions, she kicks them all out of her mansion in a temper tantrum of glass throwing. While Crane laughs and Doc mourns the loss of good Dewar's, Wharton can only moan, "The demned fool...the demned old fool" (46, 157-161).

But if he sees that the class in such extremities of behavior is absurd, the managerial detective has no reluctance about using its power in the service of his job. As representative of a member of this dominant class in a Chicago of hostile ethnic underclasses, Crane makes pragmatic use of class hostility in a labor alliance that harnesses violent criminal energy. In the opening deathhouse scene Westland comes into contact with Dave Connors, an Irish labor organizer and racketeer, with whom the broker makes a friendship that leads Connors to give Westland and Crane the services of his labor enforcers. The petty thief Mannie Grant has offered information of value to the defense of Westland; at the Club Monmarte Crane is to meet with Grant, who is unfortunately murdered in the nightclub before he can talk. The murdered hoodlum's Italian criminal associates, whose capo is Joe Petro, believe that Crane fingered Grant; therefore they attempt an assassination of Crane and Doc.

The failed attempt to murder the detectives and their later assault upon Joe Petro comprise the strongest scenes of violence in the novel. Latimer emphasizes its sources in ethnic conflict, a note introduced in the deathhouse tensions between the Irish Connors and the Jewish Verecha, and in the sadistic guard Percival Galt's underclass hatred of Westland. Walking down State Street toward the Detective Bureau, Crane and Williams become aware that from a passing car a man with a submachine gun is about to fire upon them. Williams pushes Crane to safety upon the snow-covered sidewalk and returns fire, but the violence has taken its own random victim, another of the city's ethnics, a "spruce nigger" who "was flopping around in the gutter like a hooked black bass in a rowboat." As they recover themselves, they observe that "The nigger slithered halfway up on the sidewalk, making swimming motions with his legs and arms, and then slid back off the curb into the street" (121).

Desiring revenge and believing that Petro may have the information Mannie Grant would have given them, Crane and Williams accept the labor organizer's offer to lend them the use of his own Irish thugs in a scene of violent intimidation. Though Crane organizes the assault and its brutality, he does not himself perform the work; for the relation between Connor's men and Crane is that of labor and management. Butch and Little Joe respectfully address Crane as "boss." Their Irish hatred of the Italians energizes their cruelty. Having neutralized the "dagos" and holding Petro in their control, they await Crane's orders: "Should I sock him, boss?" "Hit him," Crane says. Petro is beaten to insensibility then returned to consciousness for more questioning; and Little Joe and Butch torture more information from him by placing a lemon crusher on his hand and exerting force until Petro tells them that Mannie Grant saw Westland exit his apartment, leaving his wife quite alive, on the night of her murder. The lemon crusher has become stuck in the tendons of Petro's hand. Crane has the information he needs. That's quite enough for the managerial detective; he can't bring himself to require further torture when Butch asks him: "Anything more, boss?" (175-186).

For all the pain he orders up, Crane doesn't indulge much in self-reproach. He rationalizes violence as a pragmatic instrument. Except for making sure the African-American accidentally wounded on the streets receives emergency hospital care, the detective shows little social conscience in dealing with ethnic, class, or gender conflicts. Not innocent of powers of analysis, he does perceive causal relation between class structure and private forms of behavior. In his detective's amoral behavior Latimer invested the inner tensions of urban life realistically and unapologetically; and as agent and victim the detective himself is an expression of its energies. Additionally, Crane's continuing desire to show good job performance to his mentor Colonel Black further retards his sense of guilt, as in his squelched qualms about the uses of violence upon Petro. For this his conscious rationale is that he has a job to do, time is of the essence since Illinois Power awaits his client in the execution chamber, and, anyway, didn't Petro's boys try to murder him right there on State

Street?

The reader senses behind Crane's surface rationalizations deeper energies nudging him toward loss of control. In *Murder in the Madhouse* the energy of the Oedipal struggle between the son-detective and false-father Dr. Livermore over Nurse Evans was sublimated in the detective's efforts to create the pattern of fact that will satisfy his true father, the Colonel, and justify his repudiation of the sexual temptress. In *Headed for a Hearse* the Colonel is absent in European travel, unavailable even by telephone or telegraph for the advice and consultation characteristic of other series novels. Crane sorely misses the stabilizing advice and approval of Colonel Black; he develops a nervous headache due to the colonel's absence and speaks irritably of the need for consultation about fine points of the case, within minutes peevishly repeating his anxious wish (114, 117).

But the headache doesn't last long, and other headaches the detective suffers come not from that stress but inebriation. The absence of the Father removes the censor, and the libidinous push toward pleasure flows to the surface of the detective's life in excesses of appetite: food, drink, woman. Dad is gone; grab. In *Headed for a Hearse* there are no nay-saying old men to be considered; and the males who associate with sexy women are in age that of the detective. For Crane every what, every where is woman, and his underwear fetish teases his eyes:

Sidewalk shop windows framed women's apparel—sturdy tweeds, fragile evening gowns, soft silver fox skins, mink coats, pastel underthings that looked as though they had been loomed by a spider. Straight from the northeast, damp from the Lake, a flagellant wind whipped blood into the cheeks of passers-by. Suddenly up flung skirts disclosed shapely thighs, and flesh and garters: pink, white, and black. (91-92)

In the character of red-haired Emily Lou Martin especially are contained prurient images of delicate underthings, the vulva, and desire. In her body language she exhibits an image of sexual presentation, an image standardized through the decade's popular culture in moving pictures, magazine illustrations, and glamour shots in photo mags; that is, of the pinup girl who sits in conspicuous display and in a ceremonious crossing of the legs discretely flashes and conceals.[10] When the group gathers to confer in the Chicago City Jail, Emily Lou has a habit of such display. In the denouement of the novel she wears "silk stockings the color of ripe wheat" and perches atop the warden's desk "with her legs crossed" so that "a seductive triangle of flesh" could be seen "where the silk ended far above the knee" (281-82). It's as if the sexual tease might preserve her from Crane's revealing the truth about her: the secretly wed Emily Lou Martin and Richard Bolston have conspired to murder Mrs. Westland, engage Emily Lou with Westland in a sham marriage, and frame him for his wife's murder in order to gain the estate through inheritance.

But class identity is also significant to understanding Crane's absorption in woman. Both the light Emily Lou Martin and the dark Margot Brentino are women of the elite whom Crane perceives as trophy females, since in their images are connected sexual glamour and the display of trendy expensive clothing signifying relationship with a successful male. With each strategy meeting of the condemned broker's associates in the city jail, the two women enter with stunning changes of clothing—collectively, the scenes constitute a sort of fashion show with models on the runway—that Crane catalogues with a knowledgeable, wishful eye.

Two episodes, a luncheon at Petro's Restaurant and an evening at the Club Monmarte, bring together these women and the detectives. The rationale is that of utility and work; the men need to gather information through the innocent appearance of being likely escorts of elite women. The scenes offered Latimer the opportunity to use his marvelous feeling for Chicago detail. They also give amusing versions of comedy of manners, since the humor of these scenes works through the clash of differences in class, gender, and ethnicity. As in the garage scene of *Madhouse* where Nurse Evans and Crane drop their identities as keeper and kept in favor of playing the dating game, in these scenes the women enter into a pretended intimacy with Crane and Doc. They become for the time their dates; and the detectives dismiss their working identity to impersonate elite males, an act supported by their expense account and Crane's polish.

In Petro's Restaurant the four enjoy an experience of Italian ethnicity as if engaged in the upper-class activity known as slumming, a commercial exchange by which the elite enter into a pseudo-integration with an underclass by purchasing what they are themselves incapable of producing (jazz, blues, soul food, etc.). Latimer's slumming couples diddle themselves into a thrilled state with Petro's reputation as a former associate of Al Capone and with the restaurant as the hangout of notorious criminal types. William Crane certifies the authenticity of the food they eat in a catalogue of antipasto delights: anchovies, prosciutto, "peppery" Chianti, etc. As a recipient of all this male attention Emily Lou gives appropriate praise of the amusement and food. In turn Crane is enchanted with the confirming presence and appetite of the two classy ladies (55-61).

In their Club Monmarte date, Latimer outdoes himself in the opportunity to present comedy of manners. The club possesses the kitsch ambiance of a nightclub that affects corny imitations of things French. The entrance to Club Monmarte is made to look like the gangway to the ship *Normandie*; inside, the four suddenly find themselves in a gaudy version of Paris. With elegant form Crane orders French cuisine; and once more, as in Petro's Restaurant, with his bottomless expense account he is the purveyor of consumer pleasures satisfying to the women whose rightness of style confirms his impersonation of an elite male. To their amusement Doc Williams makes underclass gaffes of behavior and language, as in his working-class pronunciation of "trun" for "thrown" and by his confession that in California he once stopped a dope ring by killing four gangsters (which wasn't so terrible because they were "Chinamen"). Latimer's description of the funny innocent vulgarity of the floor show routines is just the right setting for the murder of Mannie Grant before the eyes of the audience, for it interrupts their bawdy pleasure with a grotesque reality that shocks the onlookers into hysterical reactions and William Crane back into his true identity as a detective (67-77).

In returning to that work Crane makes contact with the dancer Miss Hogan, in whom there is no gender and class symbolism like that attached to the glamorous, unattainable Misses Martin and Brentino. With Miss Hogan his dark distrust of women in general comes to focus. Perceiving her as fair game because she is of the underclass, she may be had without ceremony through the exchange of money for sexual favors. In his view of elite women, the explicitness of the money valuation is suppressed only to reappear in the sublimated forms of elite courting behavior (goods and services provided by the male). Miss Hogan, the working girl, is blunt of speech; she does not engage in the indirection of language used by the elite Misses Martin and Brentino. Crane is equally direct. Examining the Westland apartment about details of the murder, he follows the movements of the woman's body with characteristic erotic interest, curious whether beneath her dressing gown she wears underwear. He and the lawyer Finklestein confer about the case but wander into a discussion of why Miss Hogan has become the kept woman of the apartment manager. Finklestein says it's the "Depression....She'll toss him over as soon as some real dough comes along." In response Crane's misogyny manifests itself in cynical practical wisdom:

"I go for a gal like that....You always know just where you are. You know you have to sleep with one eye open to keep from having your throat cut. Then, when she double-crosses you, you're not as surprised as you are when a nice girl does." (110, 113-14)

Coming from one who generally places great value on maintaining an imperturbable manner, Crane's blurted cynicism shocks the reader in the overthrow of the censor and the eruption of the detective's true belief. However, his and Finklestein's reactions to Miss Hogan—at best justified as a sort of social pragmatism—exist as a median of male response in *Headed for a Hearse,* in which women victimize men and men victimize women in gender warfare carried out by female cunning and male violence. On the one hand there is Westland's naiveté about Emily Lou, which is based upon his sentimental idealization of her as a woman. He resists the truth, and Crane's explanation of her treachery sends him into a tailspin of depression (305-06). On the other hand there is the murderous sadism of the insane Isadora Varecha, a Chicago version of Jack the Ripper. After killing his girlfriend by pushing her in front of a vehicle, he goes next to a random prostitute, whom he murders simply because she is female. As he confesses to the sickened Westland: "I went up to this floosie's room, see?...an' she lay down and she was big and fat like she was with a brat, see; and I took my knife an' cut her open at the stomach" (223).

The episodes of gang violence and gender warfare are the most grotesque manifestations of the suppressed, irrational energies flowing beneath the surface decorum of events in the novel. Crane knows that if Chicago shows order and rationality, it is only made to appear that way. Latimer plays off this recognition against the premise of a rationally organized universe displayed in puzzle-mystery. Finklestein and Crane have an amused awareness of how it ought to be, but the ratiocination they carry on like the great detectives they wryly seek to emulate denies discovery (111-12). So far, their experience suggests that chaos rules, at least in Chicago.

The writer continues to play Crane's experience against the

expectations of rational understanding based upon the accumulation of clues. In ordinary puzzle-mystery the detective at some point retires into private thought to order his objects, as in Conan Doyle's secluding Sherlock Holmes at 221-B Baker Street with pipe and shag tobacco or Agatha Christie's closeting Hercule Poirot to exercise his "gray matter." Latimer's tough-guy version of that performance gives us Crane repudiating rational process, shedding the frustrations of consciousness by desperate drinking that leaves him in a numbed void of mind.[11] Going over and over the details and feeling certain that his client is doomed because he is such a miserable thinker, Crane drinks gin in Miss Hogan's apartment until he falls into a drugged sleep. Awakening, he finds that he has a renewed power of mind that seems to have come from deep unconscious sources in sleep, a state of enlightenment, he notes, that monks and saints labored to get from perverse, masochistic practices but which he received by getting really drunk. As he showers and tries to hear Miss Hogan's words over the sound of water, the eureka process occurs by which details begin to fall into order in a set of hypotheses (225-30).

Coming from his drunk-accessed unconsciousness, it is the jump start Crane needs, and now he is off to test his hypotheses in far-out acts that have the character of fraternity stunts: numerous taxi trips between Westland's apartment and brokerage office to determine the likely site from which Bolston threw a pistol into the Chicago River, the marking of the sitc ⋅ ⁊ casting into the water a tool which Crane recovers (and yes, the hypothesized pistol as well) by hiring a diver to recover them, Crane and Doc's impersonation of army officers from the Department of War when a policeman questions their presence because of the traffic jam of curious drivers (241-59). Like the antics of boys having fun, these are the comic eccentricities that captured the attention of reviewers and readers, who came to expect such behavior in Latimer's books.

Crane's final stunt is an airplane race against the deathhouse clock to confer with the gun merchant G. Washington. The detective believes that in downstate Peoria Bolston bought the Webley he used to frame Westland, and the hunch proves correct. The sole dealer in Webley pistols in the Illinois area, Mr. Washington also has a museum-like private collection of arms which he proudly shows. Among them are weapons that belonged to Wyatt Earp and Daniel Boone and a Gatling gun that would have ended the Civil War sooner, the dealer observes, if "old Abe" had been more willing to use it. When Crane points out the dealer could stock

"A hell of a big revolution," this father-of-our-country responds, "We have...We even supplied the guns for both the revolutionists and the federalists in one Central American country" (273-79). Latimer's tongue-in-cheek synoptic history seems to suggest that the violent use of weapons is as basic to American history as it is to this little piece of Chicago history.

Peoria has given him what he needs. The frantic return to the Chicago jail finds Westland shaved and trouser-slitted for the execution. Enough time, however, for Crane to unravel the knotted threads of truth and reveal the large motive of the conspiracy organized by Emily Lou Martin and Robert Bolston against the Westlands. For the detective has discovered that the common anxiety of the Depression decade affects not just the underclass but these leisured wealthy whom he wishes to emulate. The diminished income of Bolston, who has overextended himself in the showy lifestyle of pleasure and consumption that he refuses to surrender, has led him first to fraud in manipulating Mrs. Westland's portfolio and then to murder. As Westland himself had put it early in the novel, the times are hard: "If I didn't have a private income, it would have been damn tough. I'd have had to root instead of taking it easy" (35).

In *Headed for a Hearse* the fear of life without money pushes all of Latimer's characters toward compromises great and small. No one seems exempt, including the guardians of the status quo. Though Crane's acts underscore that point, it is also important to note that his success in determining the true source of criminality and saving Westland's life has the effect of expelling unworthy members of the elite but preserving its power and wealth. Westland has grown sadly aware but remains rich and in his place.

With ironic amusement Crane listens to the lawyer Finklestein's plans to take the compliant Miss Hogan on a Florida vacation. He loses again. He himself will take another assignment from Colonel Black.

iv. *The Lady in the Morgue (1936)*

In the next novel of Chicago setting, Colonel Black assigns William Crane the task of determining if the lady known as Alice Ross in the Cook County Morgue may in reality be that of Kathryn (Kit) Courtland, the estranged and missing daughter of a New York City family of old wealth. Kit's mother, Uncle Stuyvesant (Sty), and brother Chauncey (Chance) fly to Chicago to follow the course of the investigation. At stake, beyond their concern about Kit, are the provisions of a trust left by the deceased father for the distribution of his $13 million estate. The narrative is given motion by conspirators who manage the theft of the body from the morgue and murders apparently designed to frustrate Crane's efforts to find and identify the body (Latimer, *Lady*) [12].

The Lady in the Morgue extends Latimer's themes, characters, and narrative elements from the earlier novels: the tensions of class, woman as central image, money and its special force in the depression milieu, violence, and the managerial detective and his comedic eccentricity of means. Except for the obligatory denouement there is little of the formal pattern of the puzzle-mystery in this third novel, as if in the development of the writer's skill he feels less the need of those elements of form. The sense of Chicago as urban space, however, remains quite strong. As winter was the season of the city in *Headed for a Hearse*, summer in *Lady* provides the writer opportunity to consult memory for the novel's forceful concreteness of detail by which the city of that season and decade is represented: citizens sleeping on lawns, porches, and roofs in the hottest nights; the detectives' frequent bathing and change of dress to remain fresh; taking refuge in "cooled air" bars, movies, and restaurants; and the gleaming perspiration on the nearly nude bodies of taxi-dancers inside the Clark-Erie Ballroom.

The narrative structure of *The Lady in the Morgue* possesses an organic unity more satisfying than Latimer achieved elsewhere in the series novels. In part it is realized through framing chapters that link personality and circumstance intimately. The opening chapter of *Murder in the Madhouse* revealed the writer moving toward that pattern by introducing William Crane as an involuntarily committed mental patient inside an ambulance wildly careening toward the Toryville sanitarium but not yet within the sanitarium setting of the narrative proper. The physical imagery of patient-inside-the-ambulance affords meaning about the detective's subjective state: his confinement, loss of identity, disorientation, and containment by a flow of events over which he may lose control, all of it coming to special focus in Crane's first view of the sanitarium as having the perfect and untrustworthy facade of a movie set. The second novel, *Headed for a Hearse*, begins and ends with framing chapters of common site, the deathhouse scenes that establish a grim morbidity of tone spoiled only by the melodramatic and predictable final chapter.

In *Lady in the Morgue* Latimer makes a further and more complex use of the technique of framing the narrative. Here, the opening and closing chapters have the common setting of the Cook County Morgue. They achieve special intensity with their photographic and symbolic focus upon the body identified as "Alice Ross." Her isolated image locates and incorporates thematic motifs (death, disguise, madness, violence, woman, money) which reflect tensions of class and gender and the states of diffidence, levity, and cynicism by which Latimer's characters— particularly William Crane—seek control of themselves.

Adding to the development of such meaning, Latimer makes more effective use of his chosen narrative point of view, that of limited omniscience. Often, he manages this point of view in exposition so objective and summary as to seem like that of a more detached omniscience; and in some instances the point of view does shift to an omniscience by which the writer offers summary reports of the interior states of characters other than his William Crane. Such a modulation of limited omniscience eases narrative movement in time and space, but at the cost of distancing the reader from intimate contact with the detective's personality. In his own way Latimer worked toward resolving a problem common to all mystery narrative driven by a detective protagonist—the detachment of the reader from the character's inner processes. For whatever the chosen point of view, the writer must work within the necessity of moving plot toward the reader's reward of final illumination without making him fully familiar with the ratiocination of the detective's mind. Additionally, tough-guy narrative posits an alienated protagonist whose alienation the point of view must confirm without such detachment that all sense of the detective's interiority is lost.[13]

Latimer solved the problem well in *Lady*. In contrast to the framing deathhouse scenes of *Headed for a Hearse* (from which Crane is unfortunately absent), the frame of *Lady in the Morgue* gives the reader direct, intimate contact with the detective's subjectivity by making him the central percipient of meanings generated by the commanding image of the dead girl's body. Latimer's control of the framing pattern, his tight lens on the iconic image of the girl, and his positioning of the detective's sensibility in direct connection with the dominant image of the novel generates depths in Crane's personality by which to index the detective's surface glibness and the gallows humor of other chapters.

In the opening chapter the cadavers of the morgue are presented as the underclass of Chicago life, its collected victims; and through them is generated a complex perspective: reality and denial, or the fear of what the bodies represent in their nullity of class, gender, and self and the need to control the fear of nullity. This is the burden of the pervasive mixed states of the chapter: the hot winds of street life that enter the chilled room of death; the odor of decomposition and the odors of refrigeration and formaldehyde that seek to deny decomposition; the dimness of lights in the waiting room by which sight of the awful place is obscured but the stark clinic lights that blindingly reveal the corpses; a prostitute's mad laughter that filters from the psychiatric hospital next door and the sane laughter of the reporters waiting for a story.

The mortuary jokes of the night attendant and reporters establish the black humor of the novel and thinly veil their own physical decay, personal failure, and gender fears. The night man Liebman spits blood when his laughter ends in a fit of coughing. The reporter Jerry Johnson is engaged in self-destructive use of grain alcohol and water, "drinking himself to death on twenty-six dollars a week" (2). The presence of Alice Ross's body excites them to salacious discussion and to a wagering game about the identity by race and gender of the corpses in the morgue vaults—a callous game of control that fails to conceal their anxiety.

When they come to the vault that contains Alice Ross's nude body, Crane is struck by its unusual beauty, a mute, static perfection, frozen by death into the absoluteness of a photograph. It is the first of several representations in the novel of the cultural icon of the American blonde, so ubiquitous as to render the body of "Alice Ross" anonymous and effectively disguised. As detective, Crane's interest lies in *who* she really is; his inner self seems as interested in the *what* she represents—the vulnerability common to her gender:

> Alice Ross had hair the color of a country road after a long dry spell. It was too pale to be called gold and too rich to be compared with honey. Her eyelids were a delicate violet, and she had that tragic look some women have when they close their eyes. Her lips were gentle....
>
> She was slender, not with the stringy slenderness of a boy, but firmly rounded, and her skin was like cellophane....it had luster and depth, and its texture was fine. (10-11)

As with Crane, to the men surrounding it the corpse becomes a projective test of personality. The reporter Johnson sees it as lascivious object. It seems alive to the reporter Greening, who drawn to touch it pulls back his hand and expresses surprise: "Cold!" he said. "Cold." The morgue attendant Liebman sees it as the image of the trophy female identifying a success that has escaped him: "I'd be willing to trade my wife in if I could get a model like this. I suppose it'd take a lot of money to keep her in clothes, though." Crane's spontaneous response ("Plenty") confirms the detective's own feelings (11).

After the body is stolen, it becomes the object of other circles of male organization and power: the justice system, whose authority is embodied in Captain Grady and assistant state's attorney Burman; and the criminal underclass, represented in the feuding bosses Vincent Paletta and Frankie French. The crime lords believe the body may be that of Verona Vincent, wife of Paletta, then French's lover, but currently fled and gone underground as has the Courtland girl. All believe that William Crane has guilty knowledge of the murder of the morgue attendant and the theft of the body.

It is no surprise that the representatives of the official justice system and the private detective come into immediate conflict here; for they generally do in detective fiction, and for at least one reason Latimer assigns this instance. The interest of police captain Grady and assistant state's attorney Burman lies in maintaining the authority of institutions by making quick easy cases, especially when the case can be made upon a disesteemed private cop who threatens their turf. Their commitment to the rigid carrying out of the letter of the law is scarcely concealed by their bureaucratic self-interest. The private operative, especially that of puzzle-mystery tradition, often serves the more ideal spirit of the law by which justice and truth prevail, even if the letter of the law is ignored. (This is also the justification of minor criminal activity: breaking and entering, concealment of evidence, etc.) Thus in the conclusion of Agatha Christie's *Murder on the Orient Express* (1934), Poirot, M. Bouc, and Dr. Constantine agree that although all the occupants of the coach have broken statute law by conspiring to kill the American criminal Ratchett, they have carried out what the courts were unable to. Having served ideal justice, they are executioners, not murderers; and the conspirators will not be turned over to the authorities.

In contrast Crane's managerial techniques serve not ideal justice but the elitism represented by the Courtlands. As in *Headed for a Hearse*, the detective's personal identification with the class appears in his efforts to emulate its styles of appearance and consumption. His first envious, self-contrasting view of Chance Courtland confirms that (25), and his continuing gestures of brotherly bonding with this elite male/alter ego and his willingness in the denouement to excuse and soften Chance's criminal acts (including his refusal to press charges against Courtland for attempting to murder the detective!) are further extensions of his class sympathy (292).

At the service of the class of power and wealth, Crane's charismatic skills as middle manager become so refined in *Lady in the Morgue* as to see him developing an infrastructure of informants and aides, including an unofficial relationship with lower police echelons. In part such relation is afforded by Doc William's prior employment as a Chicago policeman, a note first struck in *Headed for a Hearse*. In *Lady* Doc continues to use that connection, but by this time Crane has developed a reputation as a successful manager of work. Reporter Greening in the opening morgue scene knows him for his brilliant resolution of the Westland case in *Hearse* (5). Invoking his acquaintance with Lieutenant Strom, Crane receives the trust and help of Sergeant O'Connor in looking around the morgue after the theft of the body and the murder of Liebman, this despite Captain Grady's ordering Crane off and the captain's anger with the sergeant for aiding the detective (22-23). Here and in other novels Crane shows a capacity for making helpful connections at a variety of levels of work and authority.

Significantly, the detective's managerial skill seems no product of an artificially delegated control. Crane never sanctions his own authority by invoking Colonel Black's name to that end, never identifies himself as their superior to his sidekicks Williams and O'Malley, though he sometimes observes the necessity of their commonly pleasing the Colonel. Without condescension, Crane associates with his fellow operatives on the basis of shared priorities: work, reward, pleasure. Crane, Williams, and O'Malley engage in a friendly, like-minded cooperation toward the common end, yet both Williams and O'Malley seem to realize that Crane's culture and powers of mind distinguish him as superior to themselves and that their natural function is the legwork they perform.

Indeed, Latimer's representation of the operatives' work models after social-Darwinian patterns in larger arenas of industrial management. In *My Life and Work* (1926) Henry Ford noted his policy of hiring workers and letting their natural talents, competition, and self-selection serve as means of finding place in the system. He summarized his practices by observing that in its development the Ford Motor Company did not use organizational charts and job descriptions to determine aptness for position but preferred a process by which individual talent expressed function. Ford applied the principle to basic labor, arguing that their natural work behaviors demonstrated that some employees showed themselves most talented for the assembly line, or as machinists, or as foremen. The principle also applied to management. As Ford explained it:

> One man is in charge of the factory and has been for years. He has two men with him, who, without in any way having their duties defined, have taken particular sections of the work to themselves. With them are about half a dozen other men in the nature of assistants, but without specific duties. They have all made jobs for themselves—but there are no limits to their jobs. They just work in where they best fit....
>
> This may seem haphazard, but it is not. A group of men, wholly intent upon getting work done, have no difficulty in seeing that the work is done. (92-93)

However naturally the detectives sort themselves out, when they approach the senior Courtlands, they do so as a party of employees under the sufferance of a superior class. As manager, Crane communicates his findings with the family and receives facilitating information, but the space between himself and this old wealth is large. Theirs is a blood aristocracy as was that of Miss Van Kamp in *Madhouse*. With only the bonding that unites himself and Chance Courtland does Crane achieve the sort of social parity the detective realized in *Headed for a Hearse*, in which he was identified and accepted by the habits of conspicuous consumption he shared with the Chicago elite. Though wealth remains an index of class in *Lady*, the Courtlands represent different practices in the use of money, expressed in their New York identity as the elite of philanthropy, education, and culture as opposed to the Chicago elite of crass materialism. Thus the Courtland trust names the libraries of Smith College and Princeton University as the beneficiaries of one-third of the thirteen million dollar fortune in the event of the decease of all heirs (164). As son Chance explains, the matriarchal Mrs. Courtland is devoted to charities supporting the Metropolitan Opera and other cultural and religious institutions (67).

The estrangement between Kit Courtland and her family is a product of the girl's efforts to extend her class interests into new expressions of art and culture that neither Mrs. Courtland nor Chance approves. As her brother puts it, when Kit began to spend time in Greenwich Village "with a lot of half-baked artists and writers" and "going around with a lot of unwashed Cubists and Joyceans," his sister's relation with the family grew strained. Then Kit's interest in ethnic jazz led her to the Cotton Club in Harlem and the girl's disappearance from New York City and reappearance in Chicago as documented by an ambiguous letter to her mother. Read as a declaration of suicidal intent, the letter is the basis for the belief that the corpse in the morgue may be Kit (68-70).

But an offense equal to her efforts to define culture in her own private terms is her repudiation of her class and the rejection of her inheritance. In the move from New York to Chicago Kit becomes the jazz trumpeter Sam Udoni's live-in companion in anticipation of his divorce and their own cross-class marriage. To her mother she writes a second letter which clarifies what had been ambiguous in the first by announcing that she now has a lover from ordinary life and that it is her intention to renounce the Courtland money and enter the working world: "that is why I must cut myself off from my selfish past, so as not to be tempted to give up if the going is rough" (199). Whether Kit truly means the renunciation remains uncertain. The reader is left to infer that her second letter is written at the urging of her brother Chance as a means of calling off Crane, who is coming too close to understanding that Kit has assumed the identity of Angela Udoni and may be liable to criminal prosecution when it is discovered that the jazz musician has murdered his wife. But if the uncertain motive of Kit's words cloud their meaning, the brother's attitude toward the sister is clear. He wishes to remove her from a scandal that will soil the Courtland name and restore her to her rightful position in the family, secure from predator underclass males like Udoni who exploit rich young women in the name of love for access to wealth. As the denouement reveals, Chance has analyzed Udoni's particular interests correctly (288-89).

The family member who from the outset knows the true circumstances of his sister in Chicago, Chance conspires to protect his sister and keep the senior Courtlands from learning the shameful truth. By stealing the body of "Alice Ross" (Angela Udoni) from the morgue, he hopes to avoid the true identification of the corpse that will lead the police to Sam Udoni and his lover Kit. Chance's unintentional murder of the morgue attendant incriminates him and pushes him further toward secret effort. Crane is suspicious of him but for the wrong reason. Considering the possibility that the missing cadaver may really be Kit, the detective probes the brother's financial resources, guessing that he may have money problems that could have led him to murder his sister; but inquiries show that Chance is perfectly solvent and would enjoy no greater inheritance if his sister predeceased him, since her money would go to charity. Chance's true interest lies not in money but in Kit's reputation. Desiring to restore his sister to family control, his extremity of behavior (theft and concealment of a corpse, murder, mutilation of a cadaver) has the force of an incestuous interest.

Serving this special thematic focus, Crane's identification with Chance as mirror self works within the convention of implied likeness beneath surface difference often found in the protagonist-antagonist pairs of detective narrative. In *Murder in the Madhouse* protagonist Crane and antagonist aide Charles bonded through their common violation of the rule against drinking and fears of unemployment during depression times. In *Lady* Crane achieves a brotherhood with Chance Courtland based upon the detective's efforts to drink, dress, and pleasure himself in emulation of such elite males. That is a note struck when Crane first meets Courtland concealed under the false name of "A. N. Brown" from San Diego, whose upper-class identity is nonetheless published by the taste exhibited in his tailored suit, which the detective's off-the-rack Palm Beach rags can only approximate (25). In private ways the detective serves his client very well, since beneath Crane's marginality of class he shares the male Courtland's class and gender views;[14] and certain scenes of sex comedy between Crane and Angela Udoni (Kit Courtland) dramatize Chance's efforts to control the sexuality of his sister through his surrogate Crane.

As the mirror self Crane's duty is to find the blonde morgue "lady" in the Courtland sense of the word. Any woman may become blonde; but Crane seeks the blonde Anglo female of attractive appearance *and* good breeding, not simply the blonde "lady" in its common American-English sense. The racketeers Vincent Paletta and Frankie French fail to recognize that Crane's uncertainty about the identity of the corpse comes from this distinction; they insist he knows the body is Verona Vincent and its whereabouts; and the detective is amazed by their offers of ten and fifty thousand dollars for the return of their blonde lady. As the narrative proceeds, the blondes replicate like Jane Doe: the corpse is known by the allonyms "Alice Ross" in the morgue and "Agnes Castle" in the cemetery;

it may in reality be Kathryn Courtland or Verona Vincent or Angela Udoni. Whatever her identity, it is her physical appearance as cultural icon that confers anonymity upon her. As Crane puts it, "I bet you could take the photograph of almost any pretty blonde, and she'd look something like the girl in the morgue..." (66). On that basis Chance seizes upon Crane's confusion as they examine old photographs of Kit and the cabaret dancer Verona Vincent (92-95). Not that he need do so. After interviewing hotel staff who've seen "Alice Ross," the detective summarizes for Chance: "We now know positively it either was your sister or it wasn't, or that it was Verona or it wasn't" (100).

Written as farce Crane's first bawdy meeting with the disguised Kathryn plays upon meanings generated by masks and substitutions. The detective visits the innocently named Princess Hotel (actually a resort of whores and patrons known through double-entendre as "the southside riding academy"), where the nude body of Alice Ross, a presumed suicide, was found. Like a whore's john, Crane registers under a false name and bribes a bellhop in order to examine the woman's room, where he makes observations that place under question the nature of her death. On the one hand the bellhop remembers "Alice Ross" as a cut above the prostitutes who occupy the hotel: "She was the kind of dame it takes more than two bucks to see." But by Crane's observations she appears to have been an ordinary woman. Except for a bottle of Shalimar perfume, her "beauty aids" are the advertised brand products used by most women. All her outer clothing is new, bearing the inexpensive label of the Chicago department store Marshall Field's; curiously, no shoes remain in the room (30-38).

Hearing the police outside, he escapes their attention by entering the next room via a ledge. Inside are a man and woman in bed, their anonymity compounded by their nakedness as the morgue cadaver was by hers. A drunken erotic interlude is signified in their hastily discarded clothing and "an imperial quart of Dewar's White Label Scotch whiskey." (For Crane, Dewar's indicates good taste; in another scene he chokes on embalming fluid from a Dewar's bottle.) Both occupants of the bed seem to have a Mediterranean darkness of hair and skin, and the man's body is profusely covered by black hair. Though he sleeps in a boozy stupor, the woman is awake and terrified. Fearing she will call out to the police, Crane gags and binds her, places the drunk in the bathtub, removes his own clothing, and enters the whore's bed in order to play a drunken client when the police enter the room to search for whoever has intruded upon the crime scene next door. The ruse proving successful, Crane returns "the hairy man" to the bed and makes his final remarks to the nude, bound woman: "I bet you could sell him to the zoo." and "I hope I'll see less of you sometime, madam" (39-42).

Crane soon learns that the two are Angela and Sam Udoni, and by the final chapters has made the inference that the dark-haired "Angela" is in fact Kit Courtland. (If one may become blonde, one may become brunette.) Significantly, in the comedic terms of his first experience with her, he has carried out precisely the brother's program, the dispossession of the underclass Italian male from his whore-sister's coital bed, the binding of Kit into submissive obedience, and the substitution of the detective as a symbolic sexual partner (for Crane takes no advantage). Further contacts with Angela-Kit extend the motifs of bondage and surrogacy, and the detective continues to find evidence like the Shalimar perfume and Dewar's White Label that show Angela-Kit has wealth and a taste for fine things. More importantly he comes to perceive details of her personality showing that if she has hair of the wrong ethnic color and performs work of the wrong sort, she has the good breeding of the lady he seeks.

He next meets Angela-Kit in a notorious Chicago landmark, the Clark-Erie Ballroom, where she is a dance hostess and Sam Udoni plays a "gang-o-horn" in the band. The detectives O'Malley and Crane are dumbfounded by the semi-nudity of the taxi dancers, who because of the summer heat and as sexual lure wear only bras, panties, hose, and high heels. Curiously, Crane feels distaste; he is "sobered and a little disgusted" by the presence of the women in the cross-ethnic company of underclass Filipino men and dislikes the close body contact offered by the dancer of his first selection. Finding "Angela Udoni," he senses in her a certain elegance. She dances with grace and restraint; and when she asks if he would prefer that she dance more intimately like the others, Crane tells her: "God, no!...I'm no wrestler." He identifies her perfume as Shalimar, and notices that even in her semi-nudity she maintains a certain classy poise (110-20).

A fight and a police raid interrupt their association, which Crane preserves by helping Angela-Kit escape. In the glaring elevator light of her residence hotel the two recognize each other from their earlier experience at the Princess Hotel, and Angela-Kit falls into hysterical screaming. Insisting that he has no intention of murdering or raping her, once more the detective gags and binds her into submission in her room, which is decorated with a taste beyond the likely means of a dance hostess. Crane's snooping reveals expensive clothing with Saks Fifth Avenue labels, a bottle of Guerlain's Shalimar, and a bank book with a balance of $3,251.68. Grown calm, Angela-Kit is released from her bonds and permitted to tell a story defending herself and even Sam Udoni's "adultery" with the suicidal "Alice Ross." Crane accepts her story for the time being since it seems to connect "Alice Ross's" movements with what the detective knows about Kathryn Courtland's history (120-30).

His growing attraction to Angela-Kit exhibits the detective's personal complexity. As symbolic extension of Chance Courtland's efforts to control her, Crane's sexual restraint in the Princess Hotel and the Clark-Erie Ballroom embodies both the incest taboo of the brother and the detective's own relict gentlemanly code. In his marginality he is drawn by her elitist behaviors. As the social pragmatist who knows how the world truly works, he approves her seemingly blunt and (in the illusion of the moment) underclass directness of speech, a quality that draws him generally to such women, including this lady of enigma.

While the detective's restraint draws from his complexity, the simpler sexual behavior of elite males in the novel presumes a traditional class prerogative—unrestrained access to underclass women. Having dinner at Hardings, Crane flirts with the pretty blonde Topsy, a dancer at the Apollo revue; but it's the detective she ignores and the wealthier Chance she speaks to on the basis of prior acquaintance in New York City. "She's an awful nice kid," he explains to the detective (102-05). Chance's worldliness later serves the convenience of Latimer's narrative when Courtland helps the detective escape from Frankie French's thugs; for his own bonds have been released by another prior conquest and yet another blonde, Sue Leonard, one of the dancers in the chorus line at French's nightclub (150-61).

The fullest expression of such exploitation occurs in the comedy of manners of Chapter 17, which demonstrates Latimer's special skill in handling funny, sleazy kitsch. The elite Chance provides the underclass detectives entree to a drunken, raunchy penthouse party attended by young women entertainers and business and professional men mostly over fifty years of age. A frenzied episode of pleasure seeking, it plays ironically upon the question of who controls whom in class-gender conflict, since each side seeks to control the other, the women by the coy role-playing of daddy's-little-girl helplessness and excitement, the men by being the agents of selection and pairing off (207-224). The comedy worked from such social dynamics recurs in the police hearing that concludes the novel; for it's a telling embarrassment to State's Attorney Thomas Darrow when the party girl Sue as witness shows surprise at "Tom's" presence and his official identity, having known him only as a party guy with a first but no last name (281).

At the penthouse party Crane hopes to be able to identify Verona Vincent and confirm at least that the missing cadaver is not the wife and girlfriend of Paletta and French. The detective's complex marginality gives him the personal sensitivity to determine which she is. "Miss Renshaw," the classiest woman present, smokes a cigarette in a red holder, wears diamonds, and possesses a husky mature voice. Latimer seems to wish the reader to think of screen images like those of Marlene Dietrich, Jean Harlow, or Greta Garbo:

She didn't walk....She slouched. She was a blonde and her face was coldly beautiful. Her hair was held back from a low forehead by a lacquered gold fish net; there were blue hollows under her high cheekbones; her lips were full and disdainful. She had on a lace gown which clung blackly to high breasts, thin waist, suave hips, and then, gorgeously, turned to Chinese red in a stiffened flounce exactly midway between her head and her painted toenails. (210-11)

Crane offers "Miss Renshaw" a drink. She accepts gin in large, undiluted quantities; he himself has difficulty maintaining the pace of her excess. As the two observe moonlight on Lake Michigan, he offers a poetic description which has the effect of being encoded elitist language: "Silver spray falling on a velvet blotter." Responding to the blonde lady's confusion about his meaning, he translates to standard English: "Moonlight on the lake." To this, "Miss Renshaw" provides further translation into practical underclass vernacular: "The moon's all right, if you like it....It don't make me romantic, though" (211). Crane has of course found Verona Vincent, who ironically wishes to return to neither her husband nor her lover; and once more, as with Angela-Kit, it is the detective's service to the control of the gender that sees him depositing Verona Vincent with the "correct" male, her husband Paletta.

Colonel Black's operatives therefore turn to the completion of a second line of investigation. From physical evidence in the murder of the Cook County Morgue attendant, Crane has inferred a left-handed, red-haired mortician who helped steal "Alice Ross." Finding the mortuary that employs such a person, the detectives discover him murdered and a record of the recent burial of an "Agnes Castle" who may be "Alice Ross." Linking episodes—a bar scene with a drink-cadging bulldog, jazz musicians in transcendental meditation high on marijuana—lead on to two nights of grave robbing in search of the dead blonde. Much of this has the bizarre eccentricity that Latimer's readers looked for in the series; the Crime Club editors emphasized that characteristic in advertisements and book blurbs.

The cemetery scenes generate a curious mixed mood of the ludicrous and the grotesque drawn into absurd unity. Latimer senses the special meanings of the place in adolescent development, just as in *Murder in the Madhouse* he used the sanitarium garage for a "date" between Crane and Nurse Evans. Beyond their obvious utility, garages and cemeteries offer private space to adolescents, and here for boyish adults whose behavior shows they continue to face issues common to youth. For graveyards have a cultural history as a site of teenage experimentation with sex and liquor and for gestures repudiating mortality, as in grave robbing and the vandalism of tombs, both of which are carried out by Colonel Black's boys. Their acts seem like some outrageous fraternity hazing, with Crane the haze-master. After their first night's failure (the coffin they dig is empty), it's loads of laughs the next night as Chance joins the guys and Crane leads the bulldog Champion through the cemetery, hoping the animal will sniff out where the corpse has been concealed.

The highjinks offer at best a nervous control of their fears. Latimer continues to work their exaggerated comic gestures against the moral imperatives and taboos surrounding the treatment of dead bodies. In these males' treatment of the blonde female corpse are incorporated regressive anxieties about death and sex, fears of entry into fullest adult genitality and the necessary march toward maturity, senility, and death. In the flashes of lightning Crane continues to have an impression of the corpse's face as "serene, peaceful, terrible." Their horror they mitigate by acting as if the recovered corpse were an unresponsive "date." Moving the rigid body over the cemetery wall, O'Malley embraces its waist and asks for the pleasure of the next waltz. In the car Crane moves its head like a puppet's to answer his boy-clown's questions about the weather and her muteness; and when the police stop them for running a light, they persuade them she is "stiff" from too much to drink, a confession that gets them off with a scolding from the fatherly cops (225-53).

The terminal framing chapters find the body returned to the morgue and Crane in control of a ruse designed to make Chance give himself away. The detective pretends to accept Courtland's suggestion that either Paletta or French still has an interest in the body. Waiting in the darkened morgue gives the brother one more stealthy opportunity; he will make a further effort to hide the identity of the corpse, this time by decapitating and taking the head with him after murdering Crane. With its tight focus on the sensibility of the detective as he comes into one final contact with the puzzle of the blonde lady, her head at once mannequin-like yet terribly alive in its violation, the scene achieves a horror not softened by humor or detachment. As Chance carries the decapitated head and attacks the detective, once more Crane is in bed (the sheeted gurney) with the blonde lady; and now the incestuous brother has joined him. Grappling in the darkness with his attacker, Crane's reality becomes a nightmarish set of united opposites. For he struggles with a vital body which seems to reveal itself as cadaver (the murderous brother holds poor Angela Udoni's decapitated head); and dualisms of life-death, victim-victimizer, female-male, and elite-underclass make a gnarled love-hate knot on the morgue floor:

> He swung his body so that he rolled on top of the person. His groping hands encountered long hair; thick, sticky fluid ran over his cheek, his neck. There was a strong odor of perfume in the hair. He fastened his knees around the squirming body below him, gave the hair a jerk. It moved in the direction of the jerk, something heavy bumping behind it. Simultaneously, a pair of hands found his throat....He tried to fight off the clutching fingers, but the long hair was tangled in his hands, and the object attached to the hair bumped hollowly against his chest. He tried to scream again, but the hands had tightened on his throat. The odor of perfume was strong in his nostrils. Specks of light, red and gold and yellow, danced before his eyes; a vein pounded in his head; his breath came in agonized gasps. He tossed his body from side to side in an effort to break the hold. (274)

Crane survives, changes the brunette "Angela" into the blonde Kit through the power of chemistry, and explains Chance Courtland's hand in preserving his sister's honor and the family name by concealing Sam Udoni's murder of his wife. In summary, Chance's acts reflect despair, if not obsession: conspiracy to conceal a felony, theft of a body, murder, mutilation of a corpse, attempted murder—enough for time in the slammer and certainly condemnation by the victim William Crane. The detective's cool defense and forgiveness of Chance Courtland reveal the degree to which this pair are mirrored selves; and Latimer achieves a symbolic rightness in connecting the brothers-beneath-the-skin as they struggle on the morgue floor to control the dead blonde lady in whom William Crane's desires are invested.

v. *The Dead Don't Care (1938)*

As the William Crane series grew, Jonathan Latimer developed an idiosyncratic pattern of narrative by balancing convention and novelty. Conventions—his own and those of the form—gave him contact with the reader. Novelty unfolded from maturing insight into the meanings of the characters and fictive world the writer found himself drawn toward. In the fourth novel, *The Dead Don't Care* (1938), his continued synthesis of puzzle-mystery and tough-guy pattern provides what the reader had learned to expect: the story of a classy, resilient, wisecracking detective doing his work with hedonistic pleasure and eccentric flair in life-threatening circumstances (Latimer, *The Dead*).[15] From his New York offices in the Chrysler Building, Colonel Black dispatches William Crane and Thomas O'Malley to the estate of the young man of wealth Penn Essex, who has received threatening letters. Engaged in that investigation, they find themselves in the middle of the kidnapping of Penn's sister Cam (Camelia) and their efforts to recover her.

Despite Latimer's allusion to tough-guy mode (Crane reads *The Black Mask*) (154), the novel's patterns return more strongly to the puzzle-mystery the writer moved away from in the Chicago novels. Just as the first series novel *Madhouse* collected a decayed traditional elite in its sanitarium, *Dead* gathers into the closed environment of the Essex mansion a representative social group of on-the-make types, mostly the tropical variety. The writer exploits the comic possibilities of the south Florida microcosm represented in Penn Essex's house guests. Acquainted with snobbery and one-upmanship, Crane is fascinated by the rivalries within the group, mostly hangers-on interested in Penn and Cam for their money—from the servants who take kickbacks given by household suppliers, to a blonde dancer wanna-be movie starlet, to a superannuated stage actress and down-at-heels high society couple, to Cuban political conspirators. Like *Madhouse* and *Hearse*, *Dead* also contains a locked-room mystery (the murder of the exotic Imago Paraguay). And, as in each of the Crane novels, *Dead* closes with a formal denouement lorded over by the superior detective.

If faithful readers know these puzzle-mystery elements, they also possess much of this Crane from prior acquaintance. After being beaten in a madhouse, machine-gunned on a Chicago street, and nearly choked to death in the Cook County Morgue, Crane now cruises the Land of Cockayne in Miami and the Keys. As in *Madhouse, Hearse*, and *Lady*, impersonating the elite provides an investigative disguise. In *Dead* Crane and O'Malley represent themselves as wealthy houseguests; from the Black Agency they have received a thousand dollars for expenses and a stylish Buick convertible. The Essex estate on Key Largo offers a men's mag dream of success: a marble resort on a beach with urbane guests including sexy women, a cadre of well trained and white jacketed servants, excellent European cuisine, and imported beer, wine, and liquors. (Suitably to their advertising-copy lifestyle, Crane spouts a slogan: Heineken's tastes "smoother, less carbonated than American beer") (12). Denying his work-and-wages reality, our marginal man seeks to realize his dream of industrial exemption enjoyed by the idle rich in showy displays of leisure. Performing work as with the left hand, he pursues "his occupation as a detective in luxurious surroundings among rich, congenial people"; for he belongs "to the pleasure school of crime detection" (4, 30).

Other extensions of Latimerian pattern exist. As in *Lady, Dead* deals with the problem of a great family fortune held in trust for children. Living well under handsome provisions for household and servants, Penn and Camelia nonetheless must depend upon restricted personal allowances from the Essex trust until the date set for its dissolution and the distribution of moneys. Meanwhile, they are guided by its administrator, Major Eastcomb, a stuffy surrogate father whose military rank suggests his pompous autocratic manner.

Within limits Crane and Penn are related as doubles, as in *Lady* Crane and Chance Courtland were mirror characters. Like Penn (whose gambling debts anger Eastcomb) Crane sees the Major as the censorious, pleasure-denying Father; for Eastcomb criticizes Crane for shirking work and drinking too much (28, 30), a criticism to which like a rebellious son the detective responds with more partying (34). Like the senior Courtlands in *Lady*, Eastcomb wishes to dismiss the detective. In *Madhouse* Crane experienced a similar fractious relation with the patriarchal psychiatrist, Dr. Livermore. In *Dead* details from the writer's private experience seem echoed in Major Eastcomb's military rank (the colonels in the writer's genealogy) and in the reference to Penn's expulsion from Valley Ranch, Latimer's own prep school (24).

And once more the writer gives us William Crane as the managerial detective who beneath the appearance of laxness productively structures the work of subordinates Thomas O'Malley, Doc Williams, and the new man Eddie Burns. Perhaps the best example lies in the cultivation of information from Buster Brown, Penn Essex's bodyguard. O'Malley knows Buster's record as a former professional boxer; and Crane, using that link, makes of the fighter a useful if somewhat reluctant confidant in trying to determine whether a house servant or one of the Essex visitors may be leaving the threatening notes.

And, as in each mystery, Crane comes into conflict with the official police authority, whose bureaucratic fumbling is amplified with a novel twist in *Dead* by its reference to Washington bureaucracy. A large task force of federal agents supplement local efforts to recover the kidnapped sister and arrest the extortionists. Fruitlessly, federal aircraft and boats scour the Keys in search of the Essex girl. After the ransom note is received, an operations room is established on top of the Homestead water tower in order to view the Overseas Highway bridge under which Penn Essex is to deposit the ransom. From the tower Department of Justice agent Wilson carries out the master plan, which fails despite the numbers of men, technical means, and seeming infallibility of organization. Radioed from the tower, agents in a hovering airplane are to land and arrest the kidnappers, who through a long wait never appear yet to the embarrassment of them all somehow have taken the ransom. In time Crane reveals Penn's guilt in the kidnapping; and although his sister remains endangered, with arrogance of office Wilson blandly assures the detective "we'll let you know if anything develops."

Aside from the innovation of bringing in the G-men, all this records fairly standard series fare. In *Dead* the writer does, however, find fresh meanings in the conspiracy theme, inserting layers of complicity, guilt, political intrigue, and chance beneath the initial conspiracy set in motion by the rich boy. In the series the most potent conspiracies are generally products of those born to the elite class who have a false sense of prerogative (Chance in *Lady*) or those members of a new elite who show culture, intelligence, and ability but whose profession fails to reward them with a sufficient income (a psychiatrist in *Madhouse*, a bad-times stockbroker in *Hearse*, a physician in *Red Gardenia*). As a young man on the make and as a classless professional, Crane has a special feeling for both sorts.

Experienced with this typology, Crane is predisposed toward a criminal analysis in *Dead* that begins with the current history of those closest to the family trust. Although Penn Essex has accrued a large debt in Roland Tortoni's gambling palace, the young man at first insists the debt has been forgiven and later asserts his refusal to pay the gambling debt is based upon Tortoni's crooked wheels. Major Eastcomb has recently forced an end to a planned marriage between Cam and Count Paul Di Gregario. While these events may have given Tortoni and Di Gregario cause to threaten Penn, the detective sees neither as likely to employ such an absurd means as The Eye notes, which are melodramatically phrased in slashing red ink and placed mysteriously in the young man's wallet or room while he sleeps.

Meanwhile, Colonel Black's boys choose to enjoy the south Florida life while checking out the Essex house staff and guests as the possible source of the notes. The alcoholic Sybil Langley, an aging stage actress dependent on the Essex largesse, is easily discounted; she goes about drinking for "medicinal" purposes and, as her name suggests, weakly prophesying doom. Albeit the Bouchers and Major Eastcomb exhibit the standard of British form from which Latimer draws the model of his elite, Crane knows the deceitfulness of appearance, however attracted he is by Mrs. Boucher's "lean, athletic" manner that "only Englishwomen can achieve without becoming masculine" (24, 48). Cam Essex's new boyfriend Tony Lamphier appears innocently incapable of deviousness as does the blonde singer-dancer Dawn Day. Only Imago Paraguay fails to reveal her true essence to the detective, due to the opaque layers of self she continues to reveal and her special place in the complex conspiracy that develops.

With this group Latimer once more displays his talent for comedy based on class and gender difference, popular taste, and vulgar consumption. Much of this is located in the Essex house and Miami hotels, bars, and nightclubs as the glittery live stage for the notoriously rich and the criminally infamous, as in the scenes occurring in Tortoni's nightclub The Blue Castle (51-69). The detective's sidekick O'Malley speaks Chicagoese ("trun" for "thrown") unsuitable to his elite disguise. To smooth his rough edges, Crane buys a *Bartlett's Familiar Quotations* and urges his memorizing a few pretty verses which might be used flexibly for social occasions, advice O'Malley follows by stunning Dawn Day with the poetic observation: "A lovely lady is garmented in light from her own beauty" (32-33, 53). The stripper, whom O'Malley associates with Mae West (36), challenges Latimer's ability to find fresh descriptors of blondeness. Living beyond her class, she is another sexy underclass woman presented in a variety of stylish garments (swimsuit, evening gown, lounging pajamas) and about whose use or dismissal of underwear the detective speculates (52).

From prior experience of conspiracy, within this group the detective's suspicions fall readily upon Gregory Boucher. Crane knows about men who seek wealth through controlling rich women—Miss Van Kamp in *Madhouse*, Mrs. Westland in Hearse, Kat Courtland in *Lady*. Boucher's uncertain class and Crane's prejudice against non-Anglo males further draws him to attention. Just as the underclass Sam Udoni's swarthy, hairy Italian body distinguished him as insufficiently WASPish to be a suitable lover to Miss Courtland, so does Boucher's darkness of skin and "cunning and unreliable" face with its "large curved" and "almost Semitic" nose put him out of sync with his younger Anglo wife Eve (36). Crane suspects that Boucher may have a history as a gold-digger; and the discovery he badly needs money, has even carried on a flirtation with Cam and asked her for a loan, makes the man even more suspicious in the kidnapping (133-34).

But Crane also has an impression of disjunction between appearance and reality, of staged appearances. On Key Largo everything seems theatrical, from the turgid notes by The Eye and the melodrama of Boucher fighting with the Colonel Blimp-like Eastcomb to the unaccustomed sea and sky outside. South Florida tropical nature possesses dramatic surfaces of novelty, beauty, and power confusing to the detective, who seeks to appropriate its meaning. In Key West he observes the difference between the pale tints of domestic flowers in contrast to the wild proliferation of flaming pigment elsewhere:

> The street was massed with tropical blooms; the air was thick with tropical odors. Flowers in beds beside the wooden houses were insignificant beside the explosive colors of vines and trees. Magentas, ochers, creams, ultramarines, lemons, ecrus, coquelicots, hennas made a subtropical tartan of the city. The tints were dew fresh, bright. (174)

These natural colors are reflected in the imitative decors of the Essex house (an interior decorator's palette of greens) and Tortoni's Florida-theme nightclub (shades of blue), where they seem excessive if not unnatural, the colors of rotogravure advertising and tourist brochures. Or perhaps it is not that the representations of colors are false but that in Florida nature itself seems contrived, like images from garish technicolor films. That is a question Crane seems to have from observing a sunset of piled clouds "giving the effect of a city on fire. Heliotrope smudged their bases, but the towerlike peaks were bright with scarlets, roses, salmons and oranges." The observer qualifies: "Pretty gaudy...It looks like Sam Goldwyn had a hand in it" (187).

Faced with this Florida, William Crane perceives its manifestations in alternative gestures of approach and retreat, like a fused Hindu Shiva and Parvati offering hand signals of boon and bane.[16] His responses—desire and fear—become related to the investigation itself, especially as it begins to reveal hidden agendas, of conspiracy beneath conspiracy. In the Essex house, the hotel bars of Miami, and Sloppy Joe's in Key West, the detective seeks to consume everything; and the exercise of appetite in bouts of eating, drinking, and lusting reveal his efforts to satiate the self with what the Florida world seems liberally to offer. Even Latimer's metaphors express it: a bedspread the color of guava jelly, a beach the color of camembert cheese, and the Essex swimming pool colored like lime pop, an adolescent image of fulfillment (6, 17, 35). The contrasting notes of fear and retreat from things Florida are struck in the opening pages of the novel, as Crane and O'Malley for the first time see pink flamingos, which unlike Chicago street sparrows and pigeons frighten them because they are very large and strangely pink and seem to stalk the men. "They're kind of birds," says Crane vaguely (2).

His uncertainties about category and relation grow and leave him confused about identity, and he continues the dance forward and retrograde. Simultaneously, the Essex "white marble house" splashed with the gold paint of sunset opens to Crane and O'Malley's pleasure but conceals sinister guards at windows. The servants are armed to preserve house and inhabitant; and neither the butler Craig nor Major Eastcomb gives the two operatives a persuasive welcome. Inside the mansion their clouded relation to the men leaves uncertain the true affiliations of the women; and it is significant to William Crane's male perspective that he is predisposed to view their identity as a function of association with a male patron: Dawn Day, Sybil Langley and Imago Paraguay to Penn, Eve to Gregory Boucher, and Cam to Tony Lamphier. Soon enough this analysis begins to fail generally, as Dawn Day's enthusiastic receptiveness to O'Malley seems to deny the idea of her exclusive and intimate relation with Essex, whose reputation as an aggressive womanizer also does not comport with the inagency and confusion he presents as an ineffectual if not womanish male.

The detective's gender categories have broken down. Crane solves no mystery in Following the Blondes—Eve Boucher, Camelia Essex, Dawn Day. Eve Boucher is what she seems, a charming British mannequin, unfortunate only in her relation to her husband Gregory. Cam Essex is a virginal athlete, a Florida girl of endless summer on the beach. Her tan and her command of recreational sports are indices of her bought leisure. Her unconsciousness of the pale skin she bares beyond tan lines by the exertion of swimming and her openness with the two detectives reflect her innocence of the male gaze and of controlling men through sex appeal (18-19), in contrast to the underclass Dawn Day's tailored tightness of clothing emphasizing breasts and buttocks and her coy flirting when she begs swimming instruction from O'Malley (36-38).[17]

In contrast to these innocents, the brunette Imago Paraguay offers Latimer's fullest development of the threatening dark lady. Elsewhere, the brunette is a sweet kid (Nurse Clayton in *Madhouse*), a glamorous Italian doll (Margot Brentino in *Hearse*), a dyed-black taxi dancer (Kathryn Courtland as Angela Udoni in *Lady*). In *The Dead Don't Care*, the dark lady Imago offers a problem in analysis for Crane, who first places her simply into the class of Penn Essex's sexy girlfriends. As he learns more of her, he discovers that her complex properties frustrate efforts to categorize her; and toward her as woman, he comes to feel the ambivalent desire and fear of his larger reaction to the Florida experience. Though identified as Latin, she seems in body, movement, speech, and face, of Chinese fragility and mythic beauty:

Her face was like an ivory temple mask, calm, bland, contemptuous; delicately dusted with rice powder, tinted under the eyes with blue, slashed with scarlet at the lips. The thin arch of her jet-black brows might have been made with a bamboo brush. (42)

Crane's consciousness of the female face as mask occurs elsewhere, as in Mrs. Brady's freshly madeover face after her emotional collapse in

Madhouse and in the cosmeticed visage of the deceased Angela Udoni of *Lady*. As image, the mask signifies the placative gesture of female accommodation and control; it also suggests contained suffering and knowledge, which here takes on historical dimensions of displacement and lost power, particularly as Imago embodies the conflicts between Anglo and Hispanic cultures. Her face remains a concealment and a confusion, for with a change of makeup she presents a more Latin aspect that nonetheless reminds Crane of "the painted death mask of an Egyptian princess he had once seen in a Berlin museum"[18] (96). His association of Imago with the religion of death and ancient royalty seems further extended in Imago's claim to be the descendant of ancient Mayan aristocracy, citing temple artifacts and treasures that remain in her family as proof of her lineage (100-101).

But if the detective understands something of her mask, he is less able to see unified meaning in other elements of her appearance and behavior. Imago's sexual orientation is obscured by her association with the lesbian actress Sybil Langley, with whom the exotic beauty seems intimate. Imago has a boyish body which she clothes glamorously and displays with flashes of leg that reveal a stockinged stiletto. To these unreconciled elements—the remote exotic face, the uncurvy body, the come-hither clothing, the stinger knife—Crane finds himself inexplicably attracted and repelled.

In the visit to Tortoni's nightclub which concludes with Cam's kidnapping, Crane continues to have a sense of life as confusing, theatrical surfaces. As place, the Blue Castle reifies the attraction-repulsion of the white marble Essex house. The decor of the nightclub is that of a tropical jungle under a night sky. The women are marvelously gowned and sexy; the men offer ceremonial toasts of brotherhood. But in the washroom Crane observes an argument between Major Eastcomb and Count Di Gregario (Cam's former boyfriend), who is also a patron of the nightclub. The old major's words seem preposterous clichés; Di Gregario's school English and Hispanic loftiness add to the impression of melodrama. Still, Crane can't deny it is real anger achieving catharsis when Di Gregario seizes the pistol the old man threatens him with and pistol-whips Eastcomb

across the face, across the bridge of his nose with the butt. Blood stained the major's white dress shirt, splattered on the lapels of his dress suit; his knees folded under him; his head hit the washbowl. There was a silvery bong, like the strike of a distant clock. (59)

With detachment Crane records the blood and the sound of head against washbowl as part of a set of events—soap skittering across the floor and the colored attendant moaning and slithering away from the sudden violence—that makes a disjointed and absurd tableau. His sense of unreality continues through his and Imago's incredible success at gambling (the croupier closes the wheel after Crane has won ten thousand dollars); the kidnapping of Cam as the party leaves Tortoni's Blue Castle; and the pursuit of the kidnappers in Essex's quick Bugatti, a pursuit that fails when in the excitement of the moment Penn faints at the wheel (52-74).

For the time being, Essex's ruse of a fake kidnapping in collusion with Tortoni moves flawlessly; his scam to pay off his gambling debts by extorting money from Major Eastcomb as executor of the Essex trust appears to work, even to the deception of the G-men by which they are led to believe that one of the kidnappers in a diving suit took the ransom money from beneath the Overseas Highway bridge. Although Essex succeeds in making his car-chase blackout seem more or less credible, the event still enters the detective's awareness as another of the out-of-sync acts he sees; and neither Penn nor Crane can foretell that darker conspiracies and sheer chance will enter to endanger Cam's life after the thoughtless frat stunt-kidnapping is set in motion.

Aspects of these alien energies Crane has already recorded at the Blue Castle without realizing their portent: Di Gregario's momentary loss of composure when he sees Imago Paraguay and Doc William's report that Tortoni is involved in a gang fight over control of slot machines, his muscle man having been recently assassinated (55, 57). When the Black Agency detectives track down and overpower Di Gregario at the Roney Plaza, Crane finds in him no vicious personal greed as motive for his attentions to Cam (what draws Sam Udoni to Kit Courtland in *Lady*); indeed, he has given her up since Cam told him of her truer interest in Tony Lamphier. His surprise at Camelia's kidnapping and refusal to believe until reading the Miami *Herald* account convinces Crane he has no guilty knowledge. He insists that the men and cargo ship under his control have nothing to do with Cam's kidnap. His fear upon seeing Imago Paraguay in the hotel room shocks the detective. From their angry conversation the operative discovers that Di Gregario is a Cuban seeking to organize a revolution in his homeland and that Imago is an agent of the ruling General Cabista and the Cuban secret police, as well as assassin of Di Gregario's revolutionary cousin.[19] Although Imago denies current activity as a counter-agent for General Cabista, Crane's discovery of the lethal history of her hidden "stinger" draws him to further excitement by "the peril that was so strange a part of her allure" (102-111).

Elements of chance also frustrate Penn's theatrical plot and lead it toward unintended ends. For Essex has given over the organization and control of the fake kidnapping to the mobster himself; and when Roland Tortoni is murdered in unrelated gang warfare, the thugs holding Cam on a boat in the Florida Straits await instructions that will not come. When they do learn of Tortoni's death, they will try to dissociate themselves by attempting to murder Cam and dump her body in the sea. Latimer's handling of the underworld czar's assassination is a skillful introduction of evil and terror bursting through innocent surface, of chance violating expected order. Doc Williams introduces Joseph Nelson, a towel service salesman and remote business associate of Tortoni's, whose presence in the Miami lunchroom murder site makes Nelson a fluke witness of the gangland slaying. The salesman's efforts to relate the irrelevant detail of his own life and his slow understanding of why Tortoni was distracted and unfriendly lend amusing irony to his account. Crane also notes Imago's discomposure upon hearing of the assassination (111-15).

However, his analysis of the relation of events remains incomplete. While waiting for instructions from the kidnappers, Essex's house guests continue to indulge themselves and engage in vindictive spats. O'Malley apparently seduces Dawn Day. Crane succeeds in fact with Imago Paraguay, his only certain sexual conquest after several nudges given by Latimer through the series novels, where it seems the detective's women always belong to another man or are ineligible in some way. The detective flees the sexual advances of the insane Mrs. Brady in *Madhouse* and sneaks into the garaged ambulance to play at the dating game with Nurse Evans, who is the sexual property of the patriarchal psychiatrist. In *Hearse* he and Doc Williams politely receive permission from the Misses Martin and Brentino's broker lovers before acting as the women's dates; Crane awakens in Miss Hogan's bed after an evening of drinking (did he? he didn't, says Hogan). In *Lady*, in order to avoid capture by the cops, he jumps into the sack with the nude Kit Courtland after she's been making love with Sam Udoni and, fearful of the guardians of rightful order, hopes not to be caught; with the corpse of Angela Udoni he acts out flirtation as with an unresponsive virgin and receives a scolding from the traffic police. In all of this he spouts his customary distancing wisecracks; and all these behaviors proximal to sexual experience end fruitlessly because Crane repudiates what is censorable to the Super-Ego (a mad woman, promiscuous blondes, the women of elite males, a whore, a cadaver). In *The Dead Don't Care* neither Penn Essex nor Major Eastcomb is an effectual male agent of control over the women of the house; nor has any woman before Imago Paraguay so richly combined the contrarieties of the Female Beloved for Crane as she has.

Imago Paraguay overcomes Crane's reluctance by asserting herself as agent of the seduction. The detective continues to perceive her mixed characteristics as making a "perverse appeal" (131-32); her boyish body and the stiletto tease his lust and fear. When he remarks her closeness to Sybil Langley, she denies a homosexual relation with the actress and chides his assumption that because she does not "have the large breasts, the elegant buttocks" of Dawn Day she has no interest in men: "There is no connection between la-arge [sic] breasts and an interest in the opposite sex" (140). His wisecrack in response, which asserts his own sexual orthodoxy, also suggests Crane's anxiety; and he pursues further the question of her relation to Sybil Langley. Nonetheless, when Imago offers to provide information about the kidnapping, he accepts her invitation of a late night visit to her room.

There, Imago Paraguay seduces him with rough sex. Dressed in transparent night dress, she refuses the information she has promised but returns to the issue of her sexuality. When Crane offers to leave, Imago embraces and kisses him:

> Her pointed breasts, under the sheer silk, hurt his chest. Over her curved shoulder, under her transparent robe-de-nuit, he could see the graceful curve of her naked back. Violently she released him. "You still think [I'm queer]?"
>
> "I don't know."
>
> "No?" She tore open his silk shirt. "No?" She made a claw of her hand, drew it across his bare chest from nipple to nipple. Her nails hurt like hell. He looked down, saw blood ooze from four horizontal slashes on the tan skin.
>
> "You bitch," he said. "You sweet little bitch." He pushed her back into the room, closed the door. "I still don't know, but I'm sure as hell going to find out."
> (156-57)

Considering the problem of the morning after, Latimer shifts the narrative train from the issue of Crane's psycho-sexual anxiety onto the safer main-track convention of the closed-room murder, the twist being that the detective is within the locked bedroom of the murdered Imago. For Crane awakes feeling "pretty good" and tries to arouse Imago with the warm language of recent intimacy ("Hi, babe") but finds her dead. What to do? After significant first thoughts of guilt (fleeing scandal, fleeing accusations of murder) and denial (might Imago have committed suicide in order to see him charged as a murderer [!]), he reverts to character as the clue-gathering detective and joking boyish male who distances himself with wisecracks and comic incident (though the windows and door remain locked, someone managed to poison his lover and remove his pants from the room) (158-63).

Better a dead Imago and jokes and games than further forays into forbidden spaces. His impressions of Imago open out toward dark meanings. In its more literal force as an element of ethnic stereotype her stiletto is certainly an image of threat to the WASP elite whose interests Crane spends so much time defending. She is a Miami form of the Irish, Polish, and Italian ethnicities Crane battles in Chicago. In its psycho-sexual implication her stiletto seems a homoerotic phallus identified with Imago's boy-like body and extends the notion of her as an aberrent dyke to be shunned. As a symbolism of the detective's sexual anxiety the little stinger seems not unlike a distended clitoris testing the male's ability to produce female orgasm.

But in the revelations of the denouement Latimer's detective finds the safe haven of rational explanation and assignment of guilt. It was Penn Essex, the prodigal son of wealth who as The Eye sacrificed his innocent sister Camelia in the kidnapping ruse gone wrong. It was Tortoni's woman Imago Paraguay who was placed in the Essex house to hold Penn to agreement. It was Penn who murdered Imago when, seeing the plan go bad, she planned further extortion by threatening the brother with blackmail or betrayal to the police. Detective William Crane's pointing finger of truth directs judgment, separates him from taint. Without meanness of spirit Crane's words still add up to the moral: All reaped their bane. Fatherly Colonel Black couldn't have done it so well, or with more style; and if the missing father, the deceased patriarch of the aristocratic Essex genealogy, looked down upon Crane it would surely have been with the benign smile of approval and distinct regret that William Crane was not his own son.

That is, all reap their harvest except the virginal sister Cam. Although this was the place for ending, that loose end forces Latimer to write on. But he no longer has in hand the narrative center, the Imago Paraguay who commands William Crane's inner and outer life. What follows, except for the local color of Key West, pales and falls away into disjointed and anticlimactic melodrama. After a boat chase in the Florida Straits, the fishing boat Crane has hired is overpowered by the kidnappers. Tortoni's thugs are too nasty to be believed. Bound and facing death in the sea, the suffering Tony Lamphiers and Cam as they mourn their unconsummated love are too sweet to be believed. Crane's heroics come from film cans of Saturday morning serials. Latimer's complex referential structure is here lost to the dullness of unrelieved stereotype and the writer's need for closure. Even the humor of O'Malley's managing to recover Crane's big gambling earnings from the thug Franky's body before it became shark food seems a forced, pale effort, and one wishes Latimer had taken a better look at the last pages.

vi. Red Gardenias (1939)

Red Gardenias runs off the reel with never a flickering loss of images on the screen. In economy and focus it is the most skillful of the series mysteries, and the influence of magazine serialization and the movies is displayed in its facile linear movement. It closes the five-volume biography of William Crane's life at age thirty-five, though the detective confesses to feeling a lot older and close to burnout (Latimer, *Red* 181).[20] Once completed, his last assignment will thrust him into a safe, middle-aged existence and erase his marginal identity by conferring upon him the marriage, class, and wealth he has experienced to date only through vicarious impersonations and imaginative use of his expense accounts. Suitably for a novel of 1939, the detective's success anticipates the larger history of the developing recovery from the Great Depression; his job-shift from agency detective to corporate flack is predicated upon end-of-decade hopefulness. The successful climax of Crane's aspirations and labor also coincides with the reward Latimer himself received from his series novels at the point in his career when, buoyed by their prosperity, he chose to move beyond them toward untested forms of narrative and into his new life of Hollywood scriptwriting.

William Crane's final exam takes him to the factory town of

Marchton, where the sprawling March corporation manufactures home appliances. He is accompanied by the new operative Ann Fortune, niece to Colonel Black; the two work undercover as a married couple in order to investigate the suspicious deaths of Richard and John March, nephew and son to Simeon March, the founder of the company. The old man asks the detective to seek evidence that Carmel March, widow of his son John, conspires to inherit the March fortune through assassination of the male legatees. From this given William Crane proceeds upon the last of his drunken, lecherous, eccentric investigations.

Here, Latimer's synthesis of puzzle-mystery and hard-boiled conventions remains intact. From puzzle-mystery are retained its defense of the class system, the centrality of the house as significant space, and its confidant characters, though the male sidekicks Doc Williams and Thomas O'Malley have been dismissed from the detective's immediate right hand in favor of the blonde, green-eyed Ann Fortune. Elements of hard-boiled convention also recur: the pervasiveness of criminal corruption within the class system, woman as the hub of conspiracy, violence focusing upon the detective, a denouement driven by action rather than analysis, as well as the expected number of threats, assaults, and murders.

However, *Red Gardenias* possesses little of the persuasive realism of the Chicago and Miami novels, largely because the writer's narrative models have undergone a marked shift. Its softening of detail and efficiency of story line reflect two altering influences: magazine serialization and the decade's cinematic appropriation of detective story. In drafting the novel, Latimer's prior contract for its serialization led him toward compression, verbal decorum, and a spare linear recording of episode. His sensitivity to the Hollywood venue prompted new developments of character and treatment of plot. The sale of three of the series novels to Universal Studios had certified the writer's marketability. In La Jolla, as he worked through the *Red Gardenias* manuscript, he deliberated upon the popularity of the Thin Man film series and sought to network with professional associates useful to a new career in film writing.

In an interview with Pauline Gale, Latimer recorded his dissatisfaction with editorial guidelines for serializing his novels. He complained about the tastes of the middle-class family audience for which the *Collier's* fiction editor Kenneth Littauer required him to edit *The Dead Don't Care* and *Red Gardenias*. Latimer observed that he liked his characters "tough. They drink and swear. This has to be toned down for magazine consumption and by the time I get through cleaning up my characters they sound like a pink tea social (Interview. "There's" 372).

An examination of the serialized forms of the two novels reveals special editorial practices and suggests that from the experience of editing the earlier *Dead* the writer anticipated serialization of *Gardenias* in its initial drafting as book. The effect was a novel draft that already possessed much of the decorum of the "pink tea social" desired by *Collier's*. In his study of the magazine market 1880-1940, James L. W. West III offers analysis of how several fiction writers (Ernest Hemingway, James Boyd, John P. Marquand, and others) dealt with modifications of text in moving from novel to serial. West observes that in 1939 F. Scott Fitzgerald drafted *The Last Tycoon* by writing its central seduction scene in hard and soft versions for Scribner's house and *Collier's* magazine (108-109). In like manner, in the same year and for the same magazine and editor, Latimer applied to the drafting of the novel *Gardenias* the writing strategies he had learned by editing the earlier *Dead* for serialization.

The earlier *The Dead Don't Care* had appeared in *Collier's* as *A Queen's Ransom* from December 4, 1937, through February 5, 1938, in ten installments of roughly equal length. It was profusely illustrated with Harry Beckhoff's line drawings that emphasized the modish sophistication and wit of Latimer's characters. Serialization required considerable shrinking of the book—by one-third (94,000 to 64,000 words); and a comparison of the two forms shows that on the whole the magazine redaction contracted the book in a fairly painstaking page-by-page alteration. Generally, descriptive passages (flowers in Key West, tropical nature, interiors, sunsets, etc.) are reduced by the rule of one-third. The detective's brand consciousness, basic to understanding his desire to enter the American consumer paradise, is regrettably lost through liability-wary editorial deletion of protected names (Buick, Bugatti, Heineken's, etc., become convertible, touring car, beer, etc.). Suffering little change are ethnic references (Boucher's "Semitic" look, references to "spicks," etc.), violence (the wonderfully effective indirect rendering of Tortoni's assassination), and the detectives' womanizing and comic drinking.

The differences suggest a curious system of propriety by which the direct presentation of ethnic conflict and violence are approved but other social realities are of questionable decorum. Sexual experience remains or is modified in a degree of taste that shows preference for sexual orthodoxy and implicit over explicit representation. The magazine women do have breasts, Camelia Essex's white tan lines still show where her swimsuit gaps, and Dawn Day's tight clothing continues to enhance her Mae West body; but Crane's panty fetish, Sybil Langley's lesbian interest in Imago Paraguay, and the detective's speculations about Imago's sexual preferences are cut. Most marked as a shift from Latimer's original conception is the altered treatment of Imago and her relation to Crane. Whereas the book develops her at length and in explicit terms as a sexual challenge to the detective, the serialization deletes all such treatment. She is, instead, directly presented as Tortoni's moll, a relationship left purposely more ambiguous in the novel because of Latimer's interest in developing the Crane-Imago association. Remaining true to her type as an exotic dark lady, to the serial detective she is pale thought, not sexual performance; and the whole of the book seduction in Chapter 11 (with its sadistic foreplay and Imago's poisoned-sleeping-pill murder as the lovers slumber in coital exhaustion) is erased and bridged over.

Latimer was a quick study. In contrast to the large spaces between book and serial forms of *Dead*, shorter gaps required breaching between book and serial forms of *Gardenias* (serialized from June 10, 1939, through August 5, 1939). Book length (about 53,000 words) and serial length (about 51,000 words) are approximately equal; and revision for the serialization lay primarily in simple deletions and substitutions. As with *Queen's Ransom*, ethnic references, violence, and the detective's skirt-chasing and boozing were permitted to stay more or less intact; but one must remember that from the outset representation of the Crane world in Latimer's book draft of *Gardenias* was softer than that characteristic of the series. What remained objectionable in the book is rendered more palatable by degree in the serialization. In the women's lounge of the Country Club, Carmel and Alice March have a violent argument rather than a brawling fight. Crane now drinks harsh Kentucky moonshine instead of the harsher laudanum and whiskey in Delia Young's apartment, and his hangover symptoms are much alleviated. Less voyeur as *Collier's* detective, he does not observe Delia's bralessness in Slats Donovan's nightclub nor her lack of underwear beneath lounging pajamas in her private quarters. Neither does he observe Carmel's breast, since it is not bared through the disarray of clothing that does not occur from the brawl she does not have with Alice.

But in addition to serialization, a paradigm from 1930's movies—

detective narrative become romantic comedy—also affected Latimer's treatment of material, particularly in the introduction of the woman detective, Ann Fortune. The MGM movie (1934) of Hammett's novel *The Thin Man* (1933) cast William Powell and Myrna Loy as Nick and Nora Charles in an adaptation so successful they were paired in twelve films through the course of their careers, including the six of the Thin Man series (1933-1947) ("The Thin" 3371). The films nourished cinematic and radio imitations, and Latimer makes no effort to conceal his indebtedness in presenting his upscale pair of William Crane and Ann Fortune. As Ann puts it (launching her own investigation at the Prima Dairy), she wonders "if the trail would lead her into one of those situations she had so often seen in the William Powell-Myrna Loy movies..." (58).

That Ann alludes to the MGM films, not Hammett's book, is significant. Elsewhere in the Crane series, Latimer reflects formal self-consciousness in drawing upon fiction models, as in allusions to Sherlock Holmes and Philo Vance in *Madhouse* and *Hearse*, and to *Black Mask* tradition in *Dead*; and the first novel, *Madhouse*, is a highly stylized adaptation of the fiction model of puzzle mystery. Through the establishment of difference between earlier print conventions and Latimer's book the writer shapes William Crane and his adventures toward an idiosyncratic vision. In contrast, *Red Gardenias* offers characters and events as through a camera filter: the metamorphosis of printed detective fiction into radio and film versions, which seem now to reenter Latimer's novel as another mimetic model. The result is a fiction which imitates pop film imitations of itself and produces a curiously remote and campy feel. Elsewhere (*Madhouse* and *Dead*) Latimer has used allusions to movies as a means of evoking the detective's sense of a false environment beneath which a conspiratorial reality exists. But when Crane faces the burglar in the opening scene of *Gardenias*, the reader is invited into a movie and radio secondary world of detective melodrama easily recognized by its *noir* imagery and sound effects:

> A white handkerchief masked the lower part of his face; a felt hat shadowed his eyes. He had an automatic pistol.
> "I'll take them papers," he said.
> Crane had never heard a voice like the man's. It had a resonance, as though he was talking through a piece of gas pipe. It sounded as though he had a tin larynx. His breath made a whistling noise, too, when he spoke. (13)

Crane may never have heard the voice, but Latimer (and any movie viewer or radio listener) had heard and seen the film-radio hanky-masked face and bullfrog voice by which a thug is known as a thug. The writer's early entry of this piece of kitsch into *Red Gardenias* helps set perspective upon the characters and their violence. Though comedy is a strength generally in the series novels, as in the recurrent nightclub scenes Latimer wrote so remarkably well, violence here takes on the character of movie bashings and pratfalls of the Three Stooges variety, a set of games played by Tough Guys.[21] To satisfy a wager won by Ann, Crane purchases two bottles of champagne from an offensive bartender in the Crimson Cat— one bottle for Ann and another, at the conclusion of their clever Nick-and-Nora repartee, to clobber the bartender with (155-56). It is a characterizing gesture.

Where kitsch comedy doesn't soften event, Latimer's casual treatment does. The first murders have occurred bloodlessly offstage and are presented as detached reports (the murders of John and Peter March which were made to seem accidental carbon monoxide poisonings in closed cars). Upon the current assaults and murders that occupy the markedly linear narrative the camera tends to linger only briefly or skip over. Slat's murder of Lefty Dolan (the seemingly laryngectomized second burglar of the opening scene) is reported (147). In half light Crane briefly and abstractly views the asphyxiated corpse of Talmadge March, another "accidental" death (195-96). The like murder attempt upon the patriarch Simeon March is reported, then its events reconstructed by inference (217); and a second murder attempt upon March recovering in the hospital produces a slapstick chase after a female impersonator (Slats Donovan) by the detective (244-48). In the final episode Slats Donovan is killed with an abrupt efficiency described cinematically as an action "like that in a prizefight motion picture which has been halted for an instant to let the audience see a particular punch." Latimer uses stopped action to record in laconic style that "Crane looked down at the body. It was Slats Donovan and he was dead" (264-65).

Although serialization and borrowings from film modified the fictional style of *Red Gardenias*, their effects nonetheless work with Latimer's intention in achieving an organic closure of the series. The novel sees the working out of themes the writer found in the personality of Crane through the four antecedent novels: the detective-playboy's gender anxieties, his efforts through managerial superiority to demonstrate worth to a fatherly mentor, and his desire for the rewards that identify and assimilate him with the elite.

Latimer's association of Hammett's Nick Charles with William Crane is conducive toward that resolution. As Crane will be, Nick is removed from marginality by his stylish marriage to Nora. He becomes steward of her personal security and wealth in the same way the marginal William Crane's cases develop his stewardship of elite family-house-wealth through the preservation of their women. Nick and Nora Charles reconcile their differences in witty clever dialogues, the verbal equivalents of more aggressive behaviors and the means by which the love-hate produced by their gender and class differences achieves catharsis and equilibrium. Similarly, from the outset of the Crane novels his wisecracking with women gives him a means of control in gender conflict, though catharsis and balance are never achieved except through the impersonations by which Crane comes into vicarious association with elite women or, as in the resolutions of the cases, by dismissing the women as criminal or saving them from victimage. All this defers but does not resolve his gender conflict.

Both Hammett's Nora and Latimer's Ann fulfill roles drawn from the confidant character of detective fiction. Elsewhere, women confidants enter detective narrative in work-place inferiority as secretaries who seem like wives in their nurturing, organizing, and directing of male energy. In Hammett's *Maltese Falcon* Effie Perine dramatizes her status through the grooming gestures she offers Sam Spade (making Bull Durham roll-your-owns for him) and by chastising but not repudiating him for his "extra-marital" affairs with Iva Archer and Brigid O'Shaughnessy. Similarly, Mickey Spillane's Velda scolds Mike Hammer for failure to work enough cases to maintain a desirable level of income; she is an effective nurse of Mike's recurrent bruises and abrasions; her sexuality is reserved exclusively to Mike. Indeed, both Effie and Velda maintain themselves in fidelity as one-man women, virgin-wives.

In contrast to Effie and Velda's implicit domesticity, Hammett's Nora and Latimer's Ann possess the spirit and glamour of elite women. Nora certainly offers a confidant's ear for getting out information necessary to move narrative. As agent, however, she seems the human equivalent of the dog Asta: well groomed, yappy, frenetic, and ineffectual. Of stronger stuff is Ann Fortune, another Latimer woman drawing out Crane's ambivalent fear-desire but offering a potential mate as WASP and niece to the boss (the writer delivers her fair green-eyed blondeness in a continuing series of descriptive epithet). She also possesses a promising virginal quality since she has no prior association with men and is no other male's "property," an identification leading Crane in other novels to admire but not touch.

However, as the equal of the detective in intelligence, ambition, and skills, she seems less the subordinate confidant than an aggressive self-starter who defines her work autonomously; and Latimer devotes sections of limited omniscience narrative to her as the agent of investigation. She is more organized and goal-oriented than the lackadaisical Crane, acts with greater bravery (foolhardiness, in his view) than her cautious male associate, and drives in car-chase scenes with greater panache. She does everything Doc Williams and Thomas O'Malley did, only better, but without the tacit submission, the inferiority of class and intelligence, by which they relate to Crane. Indeed, Ann threatens to out-detective the detective. Though he is attracted by her WASPish beauty, Crane feels ill at ease because of her successful entry into the arena of male work and her uninterest in traditional women's activities, a conflict that serves as one axis of the book's gender comedy.

The donnee established by the opening of *Gardenias* efficiently moves Crane toward his new life and incorporates familiar themes and motifs. Using impersonation as their investigative cover, William Crane and Ann Fortune enjoy class pleasures and corporate perquisites. As if an adoptive father, Simeon March has provided them with the murdered Richard March's former life, or at least its outer signs—a smartly modern suburban house finished by an interior decorator of note, a company car, and congenial black servants who use a kitchen furnished with March appliances. The two are also given membership in the Duck Club (a gun club), the Country Club, and presumably free medical care in the community hospital built by the March Foundation (where Simeon March recovers from the attempt upon his life). Crane's old life as employee of the Black Agency appears only in weakened form: he makes no anxious telephone calls to the Colonel for advice and consent; only the former associate Doc Williams appears in the novel, but in much diminished capacity and in a new, truer impersonation as chauffeur of the company car.

The comedy of gender conflict initiated in the opening extends throughout. It is based upon the ironic difference between the couple's

assumed and true state and the fun-and-games of role playing. When Ann
detects a burglar downstairs, she requires Crane to check it out because
that's what husbands are supposed to do. Crane finally agrees: "If I'm
killed you'll have me on your conscience." Ann jabs back: "It won't be
much of a load" (3). The first "burglar" (Peter March) spills a drink; and
acting like a good house husband, Crane worries about the ice cubes
making dark circles on the expensive Aubusson rug (4-7). When Carmel
March drops by, Crane flirts shamelessly in his role as concupiscent male
suburbanite, just as his gender opposite Ann flirts tit-for-tat with Peter
(19). Leaving for work in the presence of Peter, Crane requires a kiss from
Ann as his "little woman"; Ann does her duty but bites his lip in giving the
kiss (39).

In his treatment of William Crane's service to Simeon March,
Latimer directly locates the detective as guardian of the class system
figuring in the novel. Perhaps that function grows more sharply defined
because of its abstraction, verging upon the intentionality of a social fable.
Although the writer appears to have in mind the Chicago urban area as its
location, the patronymic Marchton seems more a city of its type as factory
town than an actual place; and March-town, as one is reminded by
responses to Crane's queries, is an idea made flesh by its founding father.
In Simeon March the detective sees the primitive energy of an *urvater*;
somehow, he looks like Theodore Roosevelt "without in the least looking
like him" (18). The gift to William and Ann of the outer forms of Richard
March's life (the trappings of affluent life that ultimately become the
detective's reward) further push the novel toward a social fable of work,
reward, and the preservation of Simeon March's system.

As a beneficent industrialist March has placed the stamp of his name
and authority on the economic and social structure of the city. He struggles
to maintain the purity of the original vision of duty and work, a doctrine
under assault by his own sons and nephews and their wives, who have
fallen into lives of idle consumption and industrial exemption. (After brief
workdays writing ads for Rapo-Arctic freezers, Crane naturally gravitates
toward these decadents, who conclude each day with early happy hour in
the Morgan House.) Simeon feels threatened also by the powerless and
moneyless professionals around him (lawyer Talmadge March, Dr.
Woodrin) and the competing ethnic underclass, here represented in the
beautiful dark lady Carmel March and the poor Irish Slats Donovan. To
Crane, Carmel is Imago Paraguay without her troubling intensity, another

one of the innocent brunettes of the series novels who wears designer outfits stunningly and whose dark beauty is heightened by its contrast to such Anglo light ladies as Ann Fortune. To Simeon, Carmel is the ethnic and female Other luring the male Marches to their deaths (after each murder, witnesses note the odor of gardenia, the strong perfume she commonly uses). As Simeon laments to Crane, with the murdered John (his son and favored heir), Carmel had not produced a grandson to carry on the family name; it was she also who corrupted the son's devotion to work. "Tie a rope around her neck, Detective. Stand her on the gallows," he charges Crane, "I'll see the trap is sprung" (27-29).

To the detective Simeon's anger seems baseless and curiously irrational, directed toward Carmel only because she is a woman and enjoys her life. His developing investigation directs him toward other events in the old man's financial past as the true source of conspiracy. His strongest lead surfaces in the history of Slats Donovan. A former bootlegger and ex-con, Slats briefly achieved legitimacy by becoming the exclusive state agent for March washing machines and refrigerators until Simeon got wind of his criminal past and fired him. After another jail term for tax evasion, Slats entered the nightclub business with Talmadge March and Dr. Woodrin, only once more to be thwarted by the industrialist's forcing his nephew to withdraw (120-21).

However, it is not Mick gangster or Wop capo that Simeon need most fear but one close to him in kind: Dr. Woodrin. A professional and social equal of the Marches, the physician needs only money to live as well as Richard and John March. His position as chief of staff at Marchton City Hospital gives him prestige "but not much money" (43). In his marginality as criminal antagonist, he balances the detective protagonist; both are intelligent, cultivated, but without means. The latter point is neatly made by the doctor's carrying a tennis net in his car—a sign of his remarkable ability in an elite sport but also of his lack, since he must often use free public courts that are devoid of nets. The net is also one of the instruments of the murders he carries out, the means by which he snares his victims before asphyxiating them.

These efforts from outside and within the class to plunder its wealth receive effective dramatization in the episode of the Duck Club hunt, to which Crane is invited and paired with Dr. Woodrin himself. It is another of Latimer's amusing glimpses of life within the class, in this instance of the relict behaviors of elite males who pursue outdoor sports, the end of which Thorstein Veblen in "Modern Survivals of Prowess" calls "reputable waste" since the ducks are collected as trophies of skill but not otherwise sought as food (258-59). Inside their duck blind Crane becomes aware that they are being fired upon by a hidden assailant, who in time is identified as Slats. In time, also, Crane perceives the irony of being coupled with the serial killer within the duck blind at the hallowed club grounds.

For the detective has begun to understand Dr. Woodrin's purpose in having accepted what seems a perfunctory trusteeship of the original Jonathan March estate (the Duck Club grounds). That acreage, the detective learns, was first settled by Great-Grandfather March in 1823 upon migration into the new land and willed as a perpetual family estate until there should be no direct male descendants, in which event it might be sold. Innocent of Dr. Woodrin's purpose, Carmel informs Crane that the tract is worth no more than five thousand dollars. But the physician's former employment by petroleum corporations in the Southwest has given him a special insight into the geological meaning of seepage in the waters of the Duck Club, the knowledge that it is an oil reserve of vast potential. (No writer's flight of fancy, this, since the discovery of oil fields in Michigan and southern Illinois during the period 1935-1945 and continuing production into the 1950s gave wealth to heirs who had maintained possession of otherwise far less valuable farm lands during the Great Depression.) Once more is emphasized Crane's stewardship of the founding vision and power of an elite clan, with which, significantly, Latimer associates from his own patronymic Jonathan and his New England *urvater* Colonel Jonathan.

As Crane resists the separate efforts of Slats Donovan and Dr. Woodrin to annihilate the Marches, it seems no forced reading of *Red Gardenias* to observe that the detective becomes the truer son and heir to the patriarch than his remaining son, the effete Peter, and that Ann Fortune and William Crane will form the next "March" generation. Though conservators of that tradition, they show little promise of offering a mindless preservation. Crane's occupational, gender, and class conflicts have moved him toward a synthesis that confirms neither the casual freedom and misogyny of his bachelor life nor the puritanical devotion to austerity and duty of the Founders. The detective seems ready to moderate his lechery and alcoholism, the vices Ann chaffs at him for possessing; and though he may appear casually attentive to duty, his record of effectiveness has always been first class.

But Crane's new estate teeters upon a fragile balance, particularly with regard to gender tensions. As revealed in the conflict between the House of March and the House of Donovan, Crane seems characteristically aroused by the sexiness of the ethnic Other, here the Irish Slats Donovan's woman Delia Young. Which is it to be, propriety and dulled passion with chaste Ann or disrepute and pleasure with bawdy Delia? In the detective's perception Delia Young transmits an aura of furtive sexual availability, like the dancer Miss Hogan in *Headed for a Hearse* or Kat Courtland in her disguise as the taxi-dancer dark-lady Angela Udoni in *Lady in the Morgue* or (most notably) the Hispanic Imago Paraguay of *Dead Don't Care*. In their dynamics of attraction across divisions of class, gender, and ethnicity such relations are given an analysis in Eldridge Cleaver's "The Primeval Mitosis" that suggests the danger Latimer's detective faces (176-90). Will Crane, like Cleaver's white Omnipotent Administrator, repudiate the woman of his own class, the Ultrafeminine, because he can find satisfaction only with the Amazon, the woman of ethnic underclass?

If their marriage works, it may be Ann Fortune's doing, since she may not so perfectly embody Cleaver's definition of the Ultrafeminine. Her lack of interest in carrying out the symbolisms of the elite woman, her personal and intellectual independence, and her insistence upon performing real work distinguish her from Eve Boucher or Camelia Essex of *Dead Don't Care*. She seems to possess qualities Crane admires in the underclass Amazons of his experience. Regardless of his snobbery and sexism, Crane admires the toughness and directness of the Miss Hogans and Miss Days and Miss Renshaws; they are victims but they are also survivors. Curiously, his admiration seems also a function of their work as entertainers, the respite they offer when as dancers and singers they remove their audience from the weary primary world into the secondary world their art offers. In *Red Gardenia* Crane feels such a personal transformation as Delia Young sings the blues in Slats Donovan's Crimson Cat nightclub. The audience, also, is so taken by her singing it is incapable of immediate applause (104-05).

Although Ann Fortune is no artist, she does share the sense of self owned by many of Latimer's underclass women. Her offer to network with an acquaintance in New York City to help the simple chorus girl Dolly Wilson secure employment as a model is testimony to her spiritual sisterhood (210). Like these women, Ann has independence and can do real work—the detective work she initiates and carries out on her own to the dismay of Crane's interest in preserving to men the work of men. His verbal shots across her bow do not redirect her course. She will not cozy up with the March women while the men do their Duck Club thing.

Doing her work in the final scene of *Red Gardenias*, she enters the cellar of the farmhouse where she believes Slats holds Delia Young. The cellar is rankly oppressive with decay, holding vestiges of the past ("a broken rocking horse, a shelf of mason jars") her self-directed acts repudiate. In the equally foul kitchen Slats assaults her. The passage emphasizes her sense of his coarse power:

> Hands clutched her from behind, bruised her breasts, finally found her mouth. The hands were strong and smelled of tobacco. She struggled, trying to catch her breath, but she couldn't free herself. She couldn't get air. The blue room became dimmer and dimmer....(213)

Ann is of course rescued, and Crane does it. Hoping that all guilt will be placed upon the gangster, Dr. Woodrin's purpose is served when Slats Donovan is killed in the assault upon the farmhouse. The detective explains Donovan's role in the copycat murder attempts upon Simeon but throws the lightning bolt of blame upon Dr. Woodrin for the remainder of the March assassinations. Feigning a possibly lethal wound, William Crane extracts a confession of love from the unbound Ann. It is a trick, and it is unfair, since he exploits her gratitude, and who can be sure how they'll feel about each other next month or next year?

Still, they have good curtain lines, the quintessential wisecracking by which this Nick-and-Nora pair balance out their love and hate. Ann searches

> ...in vain for the wound. She let go of the shirt, looked up at his face.
> "You louse!" she said. "Fooling me like that! I'll never speak to you again as long as I live."
> "Darling," he said, grinning, "then you'll make me an ideal wife." (280)

Notes

[1]For a discussion of the origins and the social implications of this pattern see George Grella's essay "Murder and Manners: The Formal Detective Novel" in *Dimensions of Detective Fiction*, eds. Larry Landrum, Pat Browne, and Ray B. Browne (Bowling Green, OH: Popular Press, 1976), 37-57. A more recent essay takes up the issues of gender and class in puzzle-mystery form: Derek Longhurst, "Sherlock Holmes: Adventures of an English Gentleman 1887-1894," *Gender, Genre and Narrative Pleasure*, ed. Derek Longhurst (London: Unwin, Hyman, 1989), 51-66. In his survey *The American Private Eye* David Geherin agrees that Latimer's plot structures borrow heavily from puzzle-mystery convention (New York: Frederick Ungar, 1985) 64, a judgment Max Allan Collins agrees with in his preface to a recent reprint of *Headed for a Hearse* (New York: International Polygonics, 1990) ii-iii.

[2]Reviews of *Murder in the Madhouse* appearing in the *Boston Transcript* 22 May 1935, 2; *New York Times 5* May 1935: 16; *New Statesman and Nation* 12 Oct. 1935: 502. It should be noted, however, that what seems condemnatory in these reviews may only be cautionary advice—a sort of rating system—for the easily offended, since each reviewer recommends the novel to those who might like the sort of book it is, regardless of its offenses to decency. Ralph Partridge's observation ("A boyish American-style book without pretension.") seems just right, an early insight into the component of adolescence in William Crane's personality.

[3]Subsequent references in this section refer to this edition.

[4]One hopes it was McCahery's enthusiasm for Latimer's fiction that led him to certain misleading and erroneous observations. In *Murder in the Madhouse* the detective is thirty-two, not thirty. McCahery's word "two-fisted" is simply not an image applicable to Crane's classy demeanor. He does not "enjoy bending an antagonist's thumb back to meet his wrist bone." Not only does he not do "it more than once," he never does it at all. (Maybe McCahery has in mind the second novel, *Headed for a Hearse*, in which Crane does become rougher, but by proxy.) Nor is his attack upon the mobster Joe Kassuccio "unprovoked," as my analysis reveals. Latimer has not always been well served by his friends, nor for that matter the writers of detective fiction surveys, as for example, T. J. Binyon's curious observation that "It is only toward the end of [*Murder in the Madhouse*] that the reader is told that Crane is a private detective who is carrying out an investigation" *Murder Will Out: The Detective in Fiction* (New York: Oxford, 1990) 41. Pity the dull reader premised by Binyon!

[5]Italo Balbo was a fascist Italian statesman and aviator who developed his country's military air fleet. His leading a flight of 24 aircraft to Chicago in 1933 would have no doubt caught Latimer's attention. The Australian Sir George Hubert

Wilkins was a polar explorer and flyer who in 1931 attempted a submarine voyage under the North Pole. See "Italo Balbo" and "Sir George Hubert Wilkens," *Encyclopedia Americana*, 1959 ed.

⁶The opening colloquy between the psychiatrists, the detective, and the two nurses is an expanded and more complex form of the opening intellectual duels of super-detective and confidant in puzzle-mystery convention. Such duels place into conflict superior with ordinary intelligence and demonstrate the amazing ability of the super-detective to pierce beneath surfaces and reveal meaning. Edgar Allan Poe's narrator and C. Auguste Dupin establish this pattern in *The Murders in the Rue Morgue.*

⁷I'm not sure what McCahery's basis is for observing that Crane, in relation to Colonel Black, "remains the individualist, his own man, not impressed by the Colonel's impatience" (McCahery 7). As this analysis shows, Crane's dependence upon the Colonel has economic, professional, and psychological sources.

⁸The story of Chicago as perceived by two journalists during the period of Latimer's tenure is told in two racy accounts of sensation and scandal: William T. Moore, *Dateline Chicago* (New York: Taplinger, 1973) and George Murray, *The Madhouse on Madison Street* (Chicago: Follett, 1965).

⁹Subsequent references in the section refer to this edition.

¹⁰George Petty and Alberto Vargas were among the commercial artists who formalized such representations in their images of the Petty Girl and the Varga Girl. Known for his advertising art and a series of posters and program covers for the Ziegfield Follies, Vargas was in demand at various Hollywood studios during the thirties, completing illustrations of set designs and promotion portraits of such stars as Marlene Dietrich, Alice Faye, Claire Trevor, and Shirley Temple (!). Vargas also had a commission for pinups which appeared in *American Weekly*, one of the publications Karl Craven reads in *Solomon's Vineyard* (3). The fetishes that appeal to William Crane seem evident enough in the iconic images such artists as Vargas had reputation for producing; and one can hardly underestimate the impact of such pervasive imagery in advertising copy, magazine illustrations, and movies. See Albert Vargas and Reid Austin, *Vargas* (New York: Harmony, 1978).

¹¹Such scenes as this prompted observations in several contemporary reviews about Crane's alcoholic excess. The ₅aturday Review called him the "drunkenest detective in current fiction" 12 (10 Aug. 1935) 14. The *New York Times* remarked that Crane "consumes unspecified amounts of absinthe, gin, and other beverages," 11 (Aug. 1935) 12. Geherin argues that Latimer introduced Crane's excessive drinking for comic effect, a persuasive argument so far as it goes, for Latimer certainly does milk comedy from it (65-66). But Geoffrey O'Brien offers a more complete analysis when he observes that the cycle of heavy drinking in Crane is like the cycle of exhilaration and depression found generally in hard-drinking fictional detectives. The end of the cycle, he points out, is non-rational meditation,

a spiritual activity "akin to the motionless sitting of the Zen monk" *Hardboiled America: The Lurid Years of Paperbacks* (New York: Van Nostrand Reinhold, 1981), 111. Crane's rhythm of frustration, collapse into drink, and recovery in enlightenment in this novel and elsewhere seems to approximate the pattern O'Brien describes.

[12]Subsequent references in this section refer to this edition.

[13]The use of a confidant as narrator, as in Conan Doyle's Watson of the Holmes stories, offers a conventional puzzle-mystery solution to the problem. Through the confidant is provided a distancing that evokes awe of the super-detective and avoids telling all yet provides enough access to personality to make him seem human. Given his creator's class system, Watson was a natural confidant; he knew the social dynamics of preferment. Of same sex and class as Holmes, he lacked only the understanding that he persistently seeks to develop and demonstrate by coming into a mentoring association with a superior male.

Since Latimer's sociology differs from that of Conan Doyle, his technique also differs. Though his William Crane mentors with the corporate chairman Colonel Black, neither of the detective's confidants Doc Williams and Thomas O'Malley mentors with Crane. His sidekicks are not social equals, as recurring comic references to their weak education and lack of taste reveal. Their friendship with Crane is based upon the common ends of their work, shared male perspective, and Crane's wise managerial willingness to meet them at their level; and the sidekicks are always the worker-muscle that facilitates Crane's manager-mind.

If Latimer's sociology helps defines his choice of narrative point of view and its limits, so does the characterization of his Crane as belonging to the class of American tough-guy detectives. Such a representation requires an appropriate technique: a restrained limited omniscience or authorial omniscience. Or a camera-like objectivity as in Dashiell Hammett's *Maltese Falcon*, by which the reader has access to interiority through inference making from objective detail, gesture, and dialogue.

[14]A vivid instance of Crane's class bias occurs in the detective's view of the coroner's jury sitting on the case of the murdered morgue attendant: "The six looked oddly alike—threadbare clothes, wispy hair, wavery eyes, smudgy skins with the water line just at the Adam's apple. They also shared a common inability to keep awake" (49).

[15]Subsequent references in this section refer to this edition.

[16]For a discussion of the mythic system Latimer echoes in Imago, see "The Meeting with the Goddess" and "Woman as the Temptress" in Joseph Campbell's *The Hero with a Thousand Faces* (New York: Princeton, 1949).

[17]Sun-darkened skin and athletic skill as a reflection of class and gender undergo an interesting shift from Kate Chopin's early feminist novel *The Awakening* (1899) to Latimer's detective novels of the 1930s. In Chopin's novel

the browning of Edna's skin and her pleasure in learning to swim reflect efforts to release herself from the bonds of class, for her elite culture emphasized skin pallor as the mark that distinguished woman's release from work under the sun, and the feminine show of physical inefficiency contrasted to male power, a cultural ritual Dawn Day plays out with little-girl weakness when from time to time she asks O'Malley and Crane to teach her how to swim. The young of Latimer's upper class pursue suntans and water sports as marks of the leisure and opportunity afforded by their identification as the elite.

[18]Certainly the reference to Valley Ranch school (Latimer's prep school) is an echo of the writer's biographical experience, and one senses that the reference to the mask seen in a Berlin museum probably comes from the writer's European travels in the summer of 1929. If so, the reference makes a suggestive link between writer and character, for the writer's association of house (hotel) with museum identifies that domestic space as the repository of archetypal woman, as Crane here develops historical and mythic associations with the "Egyptian" Imago who occupies the aristocratic house of Essex.

[19]Latimer's "General Cabista" seems an homonym for General Fulgencio Batista, who became dictator of Cuba in the August, 1933 revolution.

[20]Subsequent references in this section refer to this text.

[21]Comedy that softens violence is also to be seen in *Madhouse* and *Lady*. However, its imagery comes from family kinship (rigid patriarchs, rebellious sons and daughters, surrogate sons, etc.), not movie imagery.

Chapter 3
Patriarchs of Boon and Bane

Although William Crane's job-shift to the offices of the March Corporation left his creator without an audience-tested character, the writer's forays in new directions suggest a certain readiness to give Crane his up-and-out in favor of new faces and even a different type of narrative. As an attempt to find another protagonist and join detective story with romantic comedy, *The Search for My Great-Uncle's Head* (1937) anticipates the more successful second effort toward such synthesis in the last Crane novel, *Red Gardenias* (1939). The African adventure novel *Dark Memory* (1940) turned away from detective formula altogether and went astray in the dark continent of reader indifference and critical disesteem. Then followed the brilliant hard-boiled *Solomon's Vineyard* (1941), which presented such extremity of violence and perversity in its characters that the manuscript lingered at Doubleday, Doran until the publishers decided to reject the manuscript. Their failure to exercise first option saw Latimer abandon the security of his lengthy association with Crime Club to find another agent and ultimate publication of *Vineyard* by Metheun in Great Britain.

Solomon's Vineyard marked the end of Latimer's exclusive commitment to writing print fiction. Its troubled publication history left him with a rancor further pushing him toward film writing. With exception of the two postwar mysteries (*Sinners and Shrouds*, 1955; *Black Is the Fashion for Dying*, 1959) film and television writing occupied his career thereafter. Considering his judgment that *Vineyard* was his best work (*Megavore* 19), he no doubt felt it deserved better treatment. Its British publication left the novel relatively unknown in the United States, and its first American publication under the title *The Fifth Grave* (as a *Mystery Book Magazine* novel, August, 1946) bowdlerized much of the language that distinguished it. In his preface to the recently reprinted novel in its original form, William De Andrea calls it "one of the Great Missing Novels in the history of American Mystery Fiction" and asserts that it boldly anticipated post-war developments of the genre (Latimer, *Solomon's*).[1]

93

i. *Peter Coffin:*
The Untenured Detective
The Search for My Great-Uncle's Head (1937)

Latimer remembered *Search* as a movement in new directions which even during its composition failed to hold his interest. To avoid staling his audience with too many Crane novels, he introduced the amateur detective Peter Coffin, a history professor whose special field is the British Restoration. Colonel Jarvis Black is transformed from his role as a detached CEO into a field operative. Although his publishers saw Peter Coffin as the lead character, the writer thought of the Colonel as the true protagonist of the new series, which in the mysteries to follow would have linked Coffin and Black as confidant and detective (*Megavore* 17-18). However, no other novels followed in the proposed series.

It seems clear that his editors wanted to repackage without too much change the writer's comedic talent, which had helped so much in developing his audience. Reflecting an interest greater than Latimer's, Doubleday and Doran expressed enthusiasm for *Search* and its author, disguised under the pseudonym of "Peter Coffin," as "one of the most successful authors on the Crime Club list"; and they stressed the amusement offered by the odd-ball behaviors recorded in the narrative (Coffin ii).[2] The publisher's blurb compared "Peter Coffin" to Georgette Heyer, a British writer of historical romances and detective mysteries. An industrious writing machine, Heyer was strong as a producer of entertainments accenting humor and character but of reputed weakness in shaping suspenseful plot (Winkel 227-29). Mindful of the need to qualify the association of the two writers, the Crime Club announcement praised *Search* as going beyond the sole end of entertainment to become "a real mystery" with "honest suspense."

Beneath surface difference Peter Coffin has kinship with William Crane. Like William, Peter is a boyish, bright, and un-tested apprentice-at-life who stands outside the door of the patriarchal estate awaiting recognition and the linked rewards of wife and wealth. But whereas the question of Crane's legitimacy recurs in symbolic representation, Peter's displacement in the Coffin genealogy is presented literally. The professor's grandfather separated himself from the main trunk of the family by pursuing an intellectual career as a university archeologist, and Peter's father also followed the academic life rather than the more characteristic Coffin pursuit of wealth through business enterprise.

Considering this old family rupture, in the opening pages of the novel Peter is puzzled by his great-uncle's urgent request to attend a family reunion at his estate outside Traverse City, Michigan. The professor remembers the house from his childhood as the site of many pleasant summer vacations; as adult he has had no contact with his relative. The invitation means a long journey from Coles University in California and a belated trip from Chicago when the professor's scholarly examination of documents in the Newbury Library causes him to miss his scheduled bus trip. Unknown to him, his great-uncle has been considering a change of will by which the estate will go mostly to the younger generation of Coffins and collateral descendants, with Peter the major heir. The reunion of the young man with the patriarch excites the old family feud between intellect and materialism; but for the great-uncle, Peter's angry repudiation of a possible inheritance confirms the nephew's selflessness. In the night the great-uncle is murdered—seemingly by decapitation—and the head is missing (17-21, 27). So is the new will, the existence of which was witnessed by the venerable servant Bronson, who offers Peter his friendship and confidences but is later also beheaded by the unknown murderer.

These complications push the mystery plot forward and offer the great-nephew a field of opportunity to resolve his internal conflict between the lives of thought and action. His relatives see him as a stiff, ineffectual, and unintentionally funny academic because he lets loose such stilted howlers as "I fail to see anything of a risible nature in this situation" and "I wish to gargle before I apprehend a cold," and because his idea of a weapon for self-defense is a hairbrush (13-14, 25). Peter is ashamed of his hypochondria and cowardly behavior, and frightened by his relatives' charges that he may have murdered his great-uncle. His growing attraction to a distant cousin, Miss Leslie, makes him specially conscious of his timid, unmanly behavior.

Complementing the nervous behavior of Professor Coffin is the tone of mock gothic pervading the narrative, in which the ludicrous finds close company with the grotesque. Late at night Peter leaves his bus to walk the shore of Crystal Lake to his great-uncle's house. Across the lake he sees the dark Coffin mansion, the image from gothic fiction that found ready place in detective convention because of its implications of the supernatural, class hierarchy, genealogy, and madness. It is only Peter's fearful imagination that leads him to hear warnings in the croaking of frogs, and the sudden calls of loons startle him, but there can be no denying his sighting an escaped madman who wanders about incongruously singing a child's song. The decapitations of his great-uncle and the servant Bronson, the crone-maid Mrs. Spotswood's perambulations in a wheelchair, George Coffin's apparent sacrifice of food to the spirit of Crystal Lake, and other such details provide a series of acts within which Peter learns to handle his fears and act like a man. They also offer the absurd humor hyped by Latimer's publishers.

While with willful ignorance the country sheriff pursues the madman Glunt as the murderer, Peter develops clues pointing to an assassin within the group of Coffin kin. He also develops the self-confidence by which he hopes to become Miss Dorothy Leslie's suitor. In his one athletic talent as swimmer, he carries off a drowning ruse that befuddles and exhausts his would-be rescuer Burton Coffin, a football scholar, whom the professor considers oxymoronic. The narrative certifies Peter's self-development when he becomes the agent of capturing the madman Glunt; and through further application of his swimming skills he upsets the boat by which the real murderer, Dr. Harvey, tries to escape (266-67, 293-95).

Regrettably, Latimer's *Search for My Great-Uncle's Head* fails to develop characters or plot persuasively. The image of the decapitated blonde head of Angela Udoni locates William Crane's complexities in *Lady in the Morgue*, gives him depth beyond stereotype. In contrast, the decapitated heads of *Great-Uncle* seem little more than stage props, elements in the general melodrama. The narrative is filled with bright, chatty conversation, conceivably drawn upon the model of the novel Miss Leslie reads from time to time, Anthony Hope's *The Dolly Dialogues* (1894) (122, 124). The Dolly Foster of that loosely organized novel flits about with pollyanna questions-and-answers about the idea of the good in the domestic setting. Like Dolly Foster, Latimer's Dorothy Leslie becomes a sort of benign counselor who also goads Peter Coffin toward performance. Why she appeals to Peter beyond her service as the first love of a rather dull male virgin remains uncertain. The professor learns to appreciate what he considers the inner integrity of some of his relatives, as in the loyalty father George and son Burton Coffin exhibit to each other by falsely confessing to the murder of Great-Uncle Coffin. However, the reader must wonder about the distrust—the suspicion each must have of the other's greed—by which each considers the other a murder suspect. The reader may also remain uncertain why Peter Coffin has interest in reconciling with these Coffins and Harveys, whose major characteristics are avarice, jealousy, and hostility. Their eccentric-professor kinsman from California doesn't come off much better, as the petty vengefulness of Peter's near drowning of cousin Burton reveals. Though we may have the writer's insistence that Peter Coffin teaches at a university, it seems to be the same stock-comedy ivory tower from which the professor is sketched.[3]

The novel works better after the introduction of Colonel Black. His is a bloodless and rather detached clue gathering and ratiocination in the puzzle-mystery tradition of the haughty elite detective. Even so, he manages to reinstall enough interest to draw the reader on, and the denouement is one of those grand scenes of the super-detective finally leading us to the truth and returning the world to us the way we like it— whole and secure. Latimer's own good judgment assessed *The Search for My Great-Uncle's Head* as the slightest of his detective fiction, and there seems little reason to question that assessment.

ii. *Karl Craven:*
The Hardboiled Dick of Notre Dame
Solomon's Vineyard (1941)

Latimer's toughest tough-guy novel rests upon the history of the religious colony know as the House of David, which occupied substantial farm lands and an imposing campus-like group of buildings in Benton Harbor, Michigan, through the first half of the century. Robert S. Fogarty's *The Righteous Remnant* details its development as an extension of millenarian and prophetic religious tradition. Under Benjamin and Mary Purnell's leadership, the group of come-outers also achieved considerable material success. The House of David marketed dairy and farm produce. Its amusement park offered exhibitions, rides, restaurants, and baseball and musical performances; it was well received as a summer resort within its region. The colony's recognition at large was founded upon the House of David touring baseball and basketball teams, known for their competitive style of play in exhibition games and for the signature uncut hair and beards of the athletes.[4]

As a Chicagoan, Latimer knew of the House of David resort that drew so many city residents across Lake Michigan on excursion boats. He also knew of the scandal that grew around the leadership of David Purnell and culminated in a trial in 1927 which saw the prophet judged guilty on charges of fraud, perjury, and obstruction of justice. Despite Purnell's death soon after, the House of David found new leaders and survived through a period of further litigation during Latimer's tenures on the *Herald-American* and *Tribune*.

Confronting this historical matter, the novelist cut and pruned for his *Vineyard*. The House of David has been renamed Solomon's Vineyard and moved to the outskirts of the small city "Paulton" in southern Missouri, where the viniculture of that region and its provincial remoteness offered a plausible setting. The dissolving of families that joined the colony, the submission of private wealth to the common good, the separation of the sexes at work and in dormitories, the organization of work gangs in the fields, the description of the Solomon's Vineyard administrative buildings joined by the distinctive archway through which visitors entered, all reflect Latimer's faithful borrowings from the Benton Harbor reality.

However, Latimer's treatment reshapes the House of David leaders and invents others. Known as the seventh "Shiloh" among his followers, David Purnell exercised a sultanic privilege with certain of the colony women, mostly new members and minor children, and sanctioned his acts scripturally. From time to time his "brides" were assigned into group marriages—chaste, spiritual associations—with colony men. This continuing behavior, Purnell's efforts to conceal and justify his sexual abuse, and his refusal to return the private wealth of those disaffected who wished to leave the colony came to divide the membership and bring down the wrath of state and ultimately federal authority. Though he was a fugitive upon several occasions, Purnell avoided capture and prosecution through a network of loyal guards, escape tunnels, and concealed rooms or fast cars. *Vineyard*'s Solomon takes from the historical model his cunning secretiveness, sexual appetite, ability to excite fanatic loyalty, and success in evading prosecution; but the pathological behaviors Latimer further assigns—the grotesque ruse of self-concealment as a venerated corpse and the ritual slaughter of young women in the Ceremony of the Bride—are the writer's inventions toward generating an aura of horror. The Princess—the novel's counterpart to Purnell's wife Mary—possesses the historical model's dominating personality, but Latimer's Princess goes beyond the queenly force of Mrs. Purnell by developing a conspiracy through sado-masochistic sexual behaviors. The complicity of the corrupt lawyer Thomas McGee and the mobster Pug Banta rests upon the probability that unindicted co-conspirators from the Benton Harbor community protected Purnell and the House of David.

The modifications suggest Latimer's perspective upon the House of David, for *Solomon's Vineyard* turns toward a special fable of social corruption. The civil threat of gangsterism finds expression elsewhere in Latimer's fiction: racketeering in labor organizations (*Headed for a Hearse*); organized crime (*Lady in the Morgue*, *Dead Don't Care*); mobster efforts to enter and control legitimate business (*Red Gardenias*). In the concluding William Crane novel, Dr. Woodrin's murders of the March sons reflect the deepest menace of these criminal behaviors as Latimer seems to see them; for the physician's acts threaten a broader, symbolic dispossession of an original American patriarchy and its centrality to social organization (the oneness of March family, March Corporation, city of Marchton). That is surely the meaning of Woodrin's efforts to commit genocide upon the Marches in order to seize the original patrimony of the land and make his own fortune through transforming it into a basic modern industrial resource (lake and land into oil field).

In *Solomon's Vineyard* Latimer adapts and extends the theme of dispossession. Hired by her uncle to rescue the proselytized Penelope Grayson from the Vineyard, the private detective Karl Craven registers his impressions of civil disease and casually executed law in Paulton (another place-surname association, like that of Marchton). The streets are dirty and trash filled. A soiled and unshaven policeman shows indifference to a violation of a traffic light. Karl's taxi driver turns left at a No Left then insists upon a dollar fare though his sign advertises a maximum of fifty cents for any destination in town. The names of both hotels suggest the Arcadian theme (the Arkady, the Greenwood), but the desk clerk at Craven's Arkady is a predatory homosexual, and the elevator is occupied by prostitutes going to their assignations (8-9).

The representation of town and colony as the site of a twisted Eden is supplemented by Craven's perception of how completely Solomon's theocracy works toward a totalitarian dystopia. As in the Benton Harbor reality of the House of David, the colonists have given up their identities in private families and converted their wealth and property to Solomon's Vineyard in order to join the community and receive the benefit of salvation during the promised thousand years of peace following Christ's return. Latimer's treatment, however, fails to acknowledge the voluntarism of those entering the House of David; his detective analogizes what he sees to the looming Russian Soviet system. On first view the vineyards seem pleasant enough. But the colonists wear the working clothes of eastern European peasants, and women in large numbers work beside men in the fields at heavy labor. As Craven comes to know their behavior, the colonists seem brainwashed—depersonalized and socially programmed by the Council of Elders. Driving through the colony grounds, the detective sees administrative buildings and dormitories and

a big marble temple. That was where Solomon lay in state. I'd read about it in the *American Weekly*. They had embalmed him like Lenin and had put him a glass coffin where the people could look at him. They were waiting for the Day of Judgment, when Solomon would jump out and lead his people to heaven in a flaming catafalque. (30-31)

However, the detective's analysis remains less an abstract political critique than a study of obstacles to removing Miss Grayson from Vineyard control. Like William Crane, Karl Craven is oriented to the work product; but his is more closely the applied crude force of Crane's sidekicks Doc Williams and Thomas O'Malley as they might be without the management of Crane or Colonel Black. Craven names his priorities (Latimer's ellipsis softened the third element): "food, fighting and [fucking] women" (23). He possesses a nodding acquaintance with professional standards, a vestigial political and religious morality, but an abundance of primitive appetite, force and aggression controlled by pleasure and pain. Psychologically, he is male libido in stubborn assault upon its shell of Ego and alternately rebelling against or ingratiating himself with the novel's various Super-Egos—prophet Solomon, lawyer McGee, businessman Grayson. (Considering the detective's coy playing with pseudonyms, his truer AKA may be that of surly Caliban.)

In the privacy of the Arkady Hotel room, his crude physicality and appetitiveness reveal themselves in the ordering of a quart of bourbon, *Film Fun* magazine and "some of those others with photographs of half-naked babes," as well as an issue of *Black Mask*, variously code forms of self-gratification and toughness. In a mirror he looks at his 240 pounds of flesh and the healing of a recent knife wound from an undetailed fight (16). This darker side is reserved for assaults upon the conspirators of town and colony, and there is little evidence that moral outrage motivates his ruthlessness. Often going beyond utility, his violence achieves a grotesque, even comic, release. Some of it assumes the posturing of hominid threat-display, as with taxi drivers, hotel clerks, and bartenders; the strategy of physical bluster, for example, turns a salesman's attentions from Pug Banta's girlfriend Ginger Bolton (18-19). The madam's refusal to give him further permission to confer with the prostitute Carmel Todd infuriates him. Although the bloody assault upon the house bouncer serves the immediate end of frightening information from the madam, Karl's rage still boils; he goes into a chest-beating rampage, terrorizing the prostitutes and systematically trashing the house, paying particular attention to the destruction of the madam's expensive furnishings (89-91). His savage attack upon the jailed Pug Banta may be a tit-for-tat exchange, but the continued blows on the gangster's head pulled between the bars ("It was like a work-out with a punching-bag.") give us a Karl seized by his fury (148-49).

By a more contained technique, he manipulates the violence of others, even to the point of sacrificing the innocent. Acting as a wily trickster by heating the fires of dissension among his foes, this economy of effort pushes the job along and preserves himself from people like Pug and the reprisals he faces when he uses more direct methods. Without compunction he incites the gang shoot-out between Banta and Gus Papas that sees the burning of the Greek's restaurant, the murder of the industrialist Caryle Waterman as innocent bystander, and the unintended jeopardy of himself and Ginger (50-62). Waterman's death in the crossfire Karl justifies as useful to drawing the attention of higher authority to the corruption of Paulton; he reasons that the murder of an important man can't be ignored. The PI's divisive strategy continues in inciting Banta to murder the lawyer Thomas McGee, the conspirator behind the collaboration of the Vineyard and the Paulton criminal syndicate (139-41). On the detective's information Chief Piper jails Pug Banta, and Karl has thus cultivated these dark energies toward the defeat of the conspiracy and the release of Penelope Grayson from Solomon's Vineyard.

Conventional codes, however, nag at the detective, who feels obligated to honor his contract and show loyalty to associates. Mr. Grayson has paid five thousand dollars with the sweetener of an additional thousand for his services; Karl feels constrained to satisfy his client. Soon after his arrival at Paulton, he discovers that his partner Oke Johnson has been murdered. He dislikes Oke but feels bound by the code of fidelity to expose his assassin just as Hammett's Sam Spade in *Maltese Falcon* feels obligated to bring to justice the murderer of his despised partner Miles Archer.

Latimer's detective is also haunted by the codes of achievement and morality in his background. A Notre Dame football star, Karl failed to complete his degree, though his success on the field follows him, as in the Princess's discovery of his identity (85-86) and Caryle Waterman's recognition of him at Gus Papas's restaurant: "I saw you play for Notre Dame against Army. And later against Southern Cal....Best tackle I ever saw" (53). In another way as well Notre Dame remains inside Karl—in the penetrating little jolt of guilt he feels against the mountain of lechery built with the Princess and his agreement to help her rob the Vineyard treasures held in Solomon's temple:

> I saw lights flickering behind one of the stained-glass windows. There was a woman on the window, the Virgin, I guess; and the lights made her look as though she was shaking her head at us. It gave me a hell of a start. (116)

His sympathy for the little people may come from a relict surging of egalitarianism into his political conscience, like the flashing recall of the Virgin into his moral conscience. But more demonstrably, his advocacy of the powerless comes from the fellow suffering he submits himself to as victim early in the novel, one of the several disguises he contrives for himself as a means of control and survival. Mostly, his disguises are alter-egos of control and success. To Chief Piper he identifies himself as a collection agent of the Acme Hardware Company of St. Louis; and to Gus Papas, as Karl "in the City Clerk's office." He rents a car as businessman Peter Jensen of Fond du Lac, Wisconsin, who is later rumored to be the "criminal agent" behind the attack on Gus Papas. Karl also passes himself off to the murdered prostitute's brother as a Treasury Department agent (14, 21, 51, 105).

His signing of "Karl Craven"—his alter-ego as coward—in the guest register of the Arkady Hotel playfully belies the detective's crude physicality. In the hotel bar he seizes the sexy redhead Ginger Bolton from the grasp of a too-attentive salesman (15-20). Ginger is grateful and attracted by his macho boldness; they agree to dinner at a roadhouse casino owned by Pug Banta, the woman's lover. Karl can't decide if Ginger is using him to excite jealousy or to remove herself from the crime lord's sadistic control. His names (Pug Banta[m]) associate with breeds of fighting dogs and roosters; his clubfoot suggests the compensatory origin of his sadism. For exploratory purposes Craven plays out his disguise as a coward, accepting the mobster's jealous beating and observing his bloody attack on the prostitute Carmel Todd while her john, Chief Piper, meekly looks on (22-29).

Role-playing as coward gives him an initial insight into Pug Banta's control of police authority in Paulton. It also identifies victims—Ginger and Carmel—whose desire for retribution makes them likely confidants. Ginger refuses throughout to cooperate; she hates Pug but fears the consequences of leaving him, though ultimately she does flee Paulton. But an interview with an angry Carmel bedridden by Pug's assault gives him the information that Banta is a front man for the Vineyard, which controls the gambling, prostitution, and distribution of liquor and drugs in the city (42-46). Although Craven has no sentimental misconceptions about Carmel as a whore with a heart of gold, the loyalty demonstrated between her and her half-brother moves him. The prostitute wishes to help her brother out of his addiction, which is fed by Banta's narcotics distribution. When Pug murders her for talking too much, the brother assaults Karl unsuccessfully, accusing him of killing his sister. Surviving by cunning and force, Karl feels not anger but a merciful understanding of how the brother's despair has driven him to hazard his own life in the weak efforts to revenge his sister's murder (102-105). Though the brother errs in assigning the murder to Karl, the PI's acts *have* contributed to the death of the innocent Carmel as they did that of the unfortunate bystander Caryle Waterman. The investigator's developing compassion achieves fullest definition at Carmel Todd's funeral, which he has underwritten because there is no money for her burial. His phrase "the poor goddam whore!" (107) and his last view of her coffin reflect his hard-boiled pity:

> I took a peek into the grave. Flowers had almost covered the coffin. I thought: there goes $135. It was the first time I'd ever spent that much on a doll without getting something in return. (135)

Karl's feeling for the victimized woman extends to Penelope Grayson and the Brides of Solomon who have preceded the girl. In his early encounters with Penelope, she seems an object of analysis and curiosity; her stupor and submission to colony discipline make it impossible to communicate her true danger and solicit her help in planning escape (33, 88-89). The urgency of her need rushes into consciousness when the detective finds her tombstone and grave prepared for the impending ritual sacrifice and the names of the pitiful young victims who have gone before. His identification with her is complete; as Karl sees it: "It was a little bit like seeing your own name on a tombstone" (122-23).

Approaching narrative closure, the PI's association of himself with these victims also incorporates developments in his relations with Thomas McGee and the Princess that reveal how the flawed Craven contributes to his own victimage. He understands that the religious idealism of Penelope Grayson has led to her entrapment; but for all his toughness, cynicism, and worldliness, a curious naiveté contributes to the PI's victimage as well. His readiness to serve the respectable patriarchy, as in his acceptance of the contract with Mr. Grayson, appears also in his relation to McGee, who seems an avuncular local version of Mr. Grayson. Judged by the outmoded car he drives and his plain office quarters, McGee seems to be a common-sense small-town lawyer. He affects indignation when he tells Karl of his failed efforts to close down the Vineyard through prosecution and injunction (39). When Karl and McGee attend the annual display of Solomon's revered body, the lawyer makes loud offensive commentary ("The temple that bootleg built." "The Prohibition Prophet.") Challenged by the Elders, McGee continues to argue his statutory right to be present; and Karl finds himself in the unusual condition of embarrassment (92-99). The old man's disguise of moral outrage continues to work until Karl discovers he owns Tony's, Pug Banta's roadhouse. The detective's roused curiosity leads him to an examination of deeds in the Paulton Hall of Records, where he discovers the old man owns several illegal enterprises, including the whorehouse where Carmel Todd worked (108). McGee's interest in seeking Karl's death adds yet another meaning to the detective's identification with Penelope's tombstone as his own.

If his understanding is dulled by the old code of honoring patriarchs, Craven's curious innocence about an aspect of his own darker side—his promiscuity and compulsion toward rough sex—almost leads him to fall victim to the Princess as well. Latimer has acknowledged the influence James M. Cain's crime novel *The Postman Always Rings Twice* (1934) had upon the conception of *Solomon's Vineyard*. Cain's Frank and Cora, the coupling of sadist and masochist, are prototypes of the psyches and behaviors of Karl Craven and the Princess. The histories of Latimer's characters, however, take quite different turns from those of Cain's. Upon arrival at Paulton Karl first sees the pretty blonde woman in the train station; she has the trappings of elite identity (expensive clothing; a chauffeured limousine). She also has a sexy body and gives him an unmistakable come-on; and he is surprised to discover her high position in the Vineyard (7). With women Karl's physicality expresses itself forcefully; and, as alluded to in the near-rape of Ginger Bolton, he has a history of playing out rape fantasy. Ginger shows an interest in action, as suggested by her willingness to let Karl fondle inside her unzipped dress in their second meeting in the Arkady restaurant (46). The gun battle between Banta's and Papas's men and the flight of Karl and Ginger from the Greek's burning roadhouse have the effect of erotic arousal upon the PI. As he and the woman view the collapse of the building from the safety of a boat, he initiates rough foreplay that earns the girl's angry words and a forceful bite on his wrist. While he sucks his wound, Ginger placates him: "Next time, ask." Karl responds: "It's more fun the other way" (63-64).

His sexual bouts with the Princess give him fullest opportunity to satisfy his dark lust. In their first private encounter she refuses his kiss and requests a foreplay of blows. When the surprised detective delivers too weak a response, she punches him hard twice, drawing out his anger and power; and they engage in a slugfest wrestling match that sees drawn blood, the ripping away of the woman's clothing, and her stimulated readiness for intercourse (73-75). With each encounter this is their pattern; and although the acting out of Karl's fantasy of rape gives him great pleasure, each return to the woman's bed becomes a competitive test of his endurance prepared for with rest and gargantuan meals of ever greater protein content. History has brought him his heart's desire, but it offers a satiation that appalls. His sense of experience with the Princess becomes nightmarish and distorted; awakened by her after one of their sexual bouts, he feels

as though I was dreaming. The moonlight had changed the look of the room, made things stand out I'd never noticed before. An open closet door threw a tall shadow on the wall. The foot of the bed looked like a picket fence. There was a second moon in a mirror. I still had trouble breathing. (115)

As a professional, his rationale of behavior remains the completion of contract. Gaining the trust of Solomon's consort is a means of gathering information about the conspiracy and rescuing Mr. Grayson's niece. Therefore he enters the sexual service of the Princess, the reward for which is her proposal to make him a member of the syndicate in authority over Pug Banta and later the offer to install him as McGee's replacement.

When she also invites Karl to enter her plan to raid the colony treasury and flee before the state police close down the Vineyard, Craven can't violate his cover. With each development he finds himself edging closer to the abyss, pushed and pulled by profession and psyche, by dread and desire. It's one thing to help the Princess steal the portable cash from among the valuables stored in the vaults; his own share ($27,000) greases the act. It's another to help her cover her murder of the vault guard, for her act goes against the absolute he has announced: "We're not killing anybody....I won't go for murder, and that's final" (116). Drawn into a capital offense, he now sees that the Princess means for him to be the fall-guy for robbery and murder (144).

The final chapter of *Solomon's Vineyard* draws a grotesque scene. To halt Karl's last-minute interference with the Ceremony of the Bride, the Princess grants him the kiss on the lips she has hitherto denied. It sends him into an ecstasy that accepts her choking arms around his neck, an ambiguous act from which he struggles free; hers is either an effort to murder him or the characteristic invitation to rough foreplay. This time, when she instructs him to hit her, he does so with a force that leaves her unconscious. Carrying her to the temple, he finds the ceremony under way, the Elders intoning a litany of praise to Solomon's Bride, the white-clad Penelope Grayson lying drugged on a litter next to the catafalque containing the prophet's body. Upon the withdrawal of the Elders, Karl substitutes the Princess for Penelope. Soon, Solomon rises from the coffin and after praying at the altar murders the Princess-Bride with a sacrificial knife. Karl struggles away from the temple with Penelope, but not before returning his part of the stolen money to the treasury vault (150-56).

A tidy few paragraphs bring closure. The waiting police take Solomon into custody, and Mr. Grayson gratefully accepts his restored niece; Karl has satisfied the patriarch of light. The final conversations between Chief Piper, Mr. Grayson, and Karl Craven manifest relief; the subtext of their dialogue is self-satisfaction with the way their acts have endorsed the social good. The PI explains how the conspirators defiled authority, how Solomon murdered Oke Johnson, how the Princess accepted her sacrificial role unaware of her fate. Latimer's bitter irony, however, pervades the scene, since it was the detective who gave the Princess to Solomon's knife. The Chief's prior failure to perform his office under Pug Banta's threats appears somehow to be absolved by Craven's help in his official scourging of Paulton. Karl wants to think of himself as "a fat, red-faced guy with a scar on his belly" who helped Justice, that "tall dame in a white robe." It is a shallow rationalization of his own taint, as he is well aware. When Grayson observes that the death of the Princess didn't seem to bother him, Craven responds with self-irony that the work of a detective "toughens a fellow up" (160).

The substitution of the Princess for Penelope is the most dramatic expression of Karl's ability to serve many ends in single acts: as wily trickster to turn criminal elements against each other; to confirm in himself behaviors sanctioned by codes of profession, morality, and the patriarchal culture; and to purge, however hypocritically, his own evil. Solomon's ritual slaughter of the Brides and his murder and necrophiliac rape of the Princess reflect the incestuous cycle of gender tyranny, of the Father's recurring victimage of his own Daughters to preserve his control. The detective's willingness to sacrifice the innocent (Carmel Todd, Caryle Waterman), his rape behavior, his self-compromises with criminality and perversity—all reflect the mirrored selves Latimer gives us in this doubling of protagonist detective and antagonist criminal. It is a mirroring the writer has provided before, most notably in the Angela Udoni-Kathryn Courtland and William Crane-Chance Courtland doublings of *Lady in the Morgue*. Karl Craven's restoration of the pale virgin reinstates an appropriately chaste stewardship in the service of an appropriate patriarch and purges the detective of his own dark errors.

For the seduction of the Princess generates troubling ambiguities. Surely one sense of Karl Craven's relation to the "Princess" is copulation with a forbidden virgin—the crime of statutory rape committed by David Purnell, the Benton Harbor Shiloh, and by Latimer's Solomon with his "Brides." And is it also another form of depravity as well? Although her honorific name suggests virginity, the Princess is, after all, Solomon's *wife* of a dominating personality and a physical maturity marked by the soft fullness of breasts and buttocks suggestive of the maternal self. That horror seems to lie in the memory jarred to Karl's consciousness by one of their steamy interludes, the memory of his own loss of virginity to an adult woman, "the physical ed. teacher at Lincoln High [Chicago] while I was a junior there. It was confusing to think that" (114). Better to repudiate it, even if you become party to murder, and especially if the end is the repentant prodigal-son Ego guided by such a benign Super-Ego as that of Mr. Grayson purging those elements of self that push you toward acts as abominable as those of Solomon.

Notes

[1]Subsequent references to this text in this section refer to this edition.

[2]Subsequent references to this text in this section refer to this edition.

[3]Though the two novels, Dorothy Sayers' *Gaudy Night* and Latimer's *Search* are quite different narratives, their closeness in time (1936, 1937) and the efforts of both writers to join romantic comedy and detective narrative provide an instructive example of how through wealth of detail Sayers managed what seems lamentably lacking in Latimer's representation of academic life and personality.

[4]I am indebted to Robert S. Fogarty's *The Righteous Remnant* (Kent, Ohio: Kent State University Press, 1981) for its detailed and lucid account of the history of the House of David.

Chapter 4
The Scriveners of the House

The proximal introduction of the writer's experience into his fiction was a continuing facet of Jonathan Latimer's mystery writing. Like their creator, the new characters Sam Clay of *Sinners and Shrouds* (1955) and Richard Blake of *Black Is the Fashion for Dying* (1959) have suffered through divorces and now face the middle reaches of their lives and careers as professional writers. Clay works as reporter for the Chicago *Globe*, a newspaper like the *Tribune* of Latimer's journalism career. The fictional reporter observes the punning of a fictional Delos Parkinson, a transparent reference to Latimer's real-life associate Delos Avery. For the *Tribune* Avery affectionately reviewed his old friend's new novel *Sinners*, identifying bars and restaurants with their Chicago counterparts and suggesting the closeness of setting and characters to real *Tribune* men and women of the author's experience (Avery KF). *Black Is the Fashion for Dying* also echoes the writer's life. Its protagonist Richard Blake is a seasoned film writer (and a navy veteran). Blake is developing an association with Lisa Carson, his new-wife-to-be (Latimer dedicated the novel to his second wife, Jo Ann Hanzlik, whom he married in 1955). The mystery opens with Blake at work on a filmscript of the sort of jungle narrative Latimer wrote in the novel *Dark Memory* (1940); and the name assigned to the imaginary film is *Tiger by Night,* which is the name of a real script written by Latimer but never mounted as film in actuality (181).

Whatever the nature of connection between the writer's life and his fiction, it is clear that the Sam Clay and Richard Blake of these 1950's novels offer sharp distinction from the detached apprentices-at-life William Crane and Peter Coffin and the wary loner Karl Craven of Latimer's prewar fiction. Sam Clay and Richard Blake have breached the solitary male life and narrow association with other male professionals in favor of a more complete and sustaining social matrix, and the result is a fiction that generates a rich sense of multi-dimensional life. Sam Clay has made warm human connection with Tom and Camille Nichols; Richard Blake's associations with Josh Gordon and Lisa Carson run deeper than

109

those of the studio workplace. These social bondings help preserve Clay and Blake from the assaults against self-esteem offered them by the managers and institutions they serve, as well as from their own fears of inner taint and failure. The critical effect of divorce for each is inward examination and heightened consciousness of their association with the institutions of journalism and the movie industry to which they have devoted their lives.

Victims of false charges, Clay and Blake become detectives because they must in order to survive; as employees made scapegoats by a newspaper publisher and studio head, they become fall guys for murders they did not commit. Their character types have precedence in detective fiction in the similar victimage of Richard Hannay, the protagonist of John Buchan's *The Thirty-Nine Steps* (1915). The more immediate source, however, was the George Stroud of Kenneth Fearing's *The Big Clock* (1946), which Latimer scripted for Paramount Studios in its 1948 production. One of ten collaborations between the studio writer and the director John Farrow, it was the film of Latimer's career with which he took deepest satisfaction. *The Big Clock* continued its hold upon the conception and development of these valedictory detective novels, not as imitative homages but because Fearing's novel held elements congenial to the organic development of Latimer's detective myth, elements present from the earliest William Crane stories: the association of families of power with the physical image of the house, the organization of work and reward around the house, and the fear and desire of those who enter the system it contains. As the writer's myth grew, the house image became more directly referential to the larger social and economic order, finding fullest expression in the patriarch/industrialism/social ordering (Simeon March/March Corporation/Marchton) of the final series novel, *Red Gardenias*. The Coffin patriarch/estate/patrimony association of *The Search for My Great-Uncle's Head* and the Solomon/temple/treasury connections of *Solomon's Vineyard* are further expressions of these relationships. The professionals of Latimer's postwar fiction do their work in corporate houses identified with the enterprise and names of the powerful founders, as in Latimer's life the Tribune Tower became associated with the McCormick family and movie studios with such names as Samuel Goldwyn, Louis Mayer, and Jack Warner.

i. *Sam Clay:*
The Detective at the City Desk
Sinners and Shrouds (1955)

Having completed the final dissolution of his marriage, Sam Clay goes on a drinking binge so desperate that when he awakens in a Chicago Northside apartment in bed with the nude body of a murdered young blonde, his alcoholic blackout has removed most memory of the past several hours, how he came to be present in a strange apartment and the identity of the victim. His lack of knowledge and control caused by the memory loss terrifies him; the savagery of the murder reflects an awful rage he can't be sure he was incapable of, given the anger he has held against his former wife and despite his inner denial of such possibility. He flees from the apartment house to his own, where he finds a bloody towel and an expensive bracelet that matches a diamond and sapphire clip in the dead girl's place. A neighbor asks him innocently why, wearing some kind of cloak, he abruptly entered and left his apartment at five o'clock. A continuing strand of such discovery about his forgotten acts gives him a frightening notion of possession by a double, "like hearing about someone else, a brother or someone, who'd got himself into bad trouble" (Latimer, *Sinners* 15).

Fleeing to his friends Camille and Tom Nichols, the three set in motion a plan to trace out his actions of the previous night; Tom also contacts the private detective Amos Bundy. At the same time the reporter is called to the service of the *Globe* in its coverage of what is believed to be a sensational rape-murder. The identification of the corpse as Mary Trevor, a new hire as a *Globe* society-page reporter, places special burden upon the newspaper staff to find the murderer of one of their own; and Sam finds himself in a position of responsibility for gathering information about a killer who would seem to be himself. Pursuing the relation of Mary Trevor to employees of the *Globe*, he also becomes its historian, since the young woman's life proves to be intimately bound to its personnel and institutional growth.

Certainly, Latimer's fictional given borrows elements of *The Big Clock*. Fearing's novel narrates the jealous murder of Pauline Delos by Earl Janoth, the powerful and charismatic director of Janoth Enterprises, a giant communications corporation of interrelated magazines and editorial staffs, all housed in a skyscraper topped by a big clock. Janoth is unaware that his rival in love is George Stroud, the editor of one of his own successful magazines *Crimeways*. Seeking to divert blame to this unknown competitor, Janoth appoints Stroud himself to head a dragnet of employees to carry out an investigation; and Stroud has the tricky job of making the task force efforts seem genuine, avoiding false charges against himself, and bringing the corporate CEO to justice.

Though Latimer retains the thriller element of suspense, many changes mark the adaptation of this basic plot to *Sinners and Shrouds*, among them the metamorphosis of Fearing's victim (a mature and rather tough-minded career woman) into the more vulnerable Mary Trevor, the demotion of Sam Clay to a reporter's role in the investigation, and (unlike Fearing's Stroud) Clay's initial ignorance of who the real murderer is. Choosing a more realistic representation, Latimer dismisses Fearing's heavily expressionist introduction of symbol and character, particularly the recurrence of the Janoth Tower and its great clock as symbol of the modern corporate behemoth that controls and destroys the individual. Only Chapter 20 of *Sinners* possesses the essential modality of *The Big Clock*; there—in the recurrence of the loud public address voices commanding the capture of Sam Clay, the sound of alarm bells, and the closing of automatic doors—the reporter seems pursued by a vindictive, personified Chicago *Globe* building.

Latimer's genius in *Sinners* lay in finding a more natural means inherent in his material of representing the element of mystery in the murder, the immanence of the past in current events, a theme he often connects with familial kinships in such sets of antitheses as real/ pretended, revealed/concealed, blood legitimacies/spiritual legitimacies. Here Latimer found means of communicating the enigma of the past in the stock-in-trade of journalism, language itself and its teasing, proximal relation to truth. Recurrently, the past shows itself to Sam Clay in signifying structures that have the effect of containing encrypted meaning; the mystery of Mary Trevor's death reveals itself in coded messages whose keys he must master. The motif first appears in his confused pocket junk retained from the wild night and the notes Sam makes of his few memories from the blackout; the absence of chronology and causality makes them disconnected signs, absurd nonsense (24-25). In a variety of forms testifying to the writer's remarkable inventiveness, the motif of encoding and decoding recurs throughout, concluding with the scene of a telephone recorder in rewind offering a reversed chaos of voices until playback links voice with speaker and puts the *Globe* publisher Mrs.

Cornelia Palmer incriminatingly in the apartment of the murder victim Mary Trevor (244-45).

In *Sinners* flawed messengers, deceit intended or not, are often the agents of encrypted meaning. The more innocent are those whose neuroses produce seeming gibberish. Clay himself is one of these, truth left undeliverable by his alcoholic lapse. A hunchback beggar—a religious fanatic who has seen a hooded intruder leave the girl's apartment—mouths biblical phrases of uncertain signification: "Jezebel. Woman of sin. The Angel of the Lord" (42-43). Mary Trevor's African-American maid Clarissa Simpson moonlights as whore and blots out self-pity and disgust by surrendering to the cruelties of her pimp and the drug-and-booze stupor out of which she delivers to Clay the mumbled report that the person who gave her a hundred dollars for the use of Mary Trevor's apartment key was a "Numb." Sam finally gets it, further evidence that someone improbably dressed like a nun was involved in the murder (200-206).

Like these, the upper hierarchy of the *Globe* staff also comprise a collection of the neurotic walking wounded. However, covering their private tics with the appearance of stable authority, they intend their evasive encodings designed to preserve themselves and the institution they serve. Among them are the managing editor Edwin Justin Standish, a health-food addict who fumbles for dropped almonds on his office rug. The city editor Harry Canning has engaged in office warfare with Standish by competing for the sexual favors of the murder victim Mary Trevor, a private history Clay uncovers soon enough. With the neutral clinical term *satyriasis*, Standish appears to find justification for his compulsive promiscuity with Mary Trevor, his secretary Miss Bentley, the mistress he keeps in the near northside, and the casual pickups that come his way: "So I got it....Now let's get on with the business at hand" (78). As managers of a great social instrument of information, Standish and Canning participate in the big lie when they send off the reporting staff to find a *pervert* and *rapist* though the autopsy report makes clear there was no rape. When Sam traces the call he remembers receiving at the murdered woman's apartment to the unlisted Washington number of the publisher, the editors divert Clay away from Mrs. Palmer by informing him that Dupont 7-7689 signifies the White House (75). It is, of course, another obfuscation, an ironic defense of the journalistic instrument of truth over truth itself.

On the way to discovery Sam Clay continues to have experiences of notes, anecdotes, pieces of conversation, a western song, old newspaper accounts, long-distance telephone conversations, a deposition, all of which deliver to the reporter an impression of encrypted subtext he has limited access to. Receiving the report that during his blackout he may have married a certain Pat Bruce, he enters her apartment and finds a message-riddle: "Cleo—Love Nest for Passion fruit. Walpurg night! Cool, girl, cool! Rendez-me soonest! Pat" (65). Its assumptions understood, it assumes syntax, and Clay pushes on to a homosexual bar in his continuing search. A bad long-distance connection and an Oklahoma orphanage director's poorly fitting dentures deliver Clay what sounds like "Auto bubbly thurbly how!" before the director begins to make more sense by offering fragments of information helpful to solving the larger puzzle (208). In all of this Sam finds himself collecting pieces of language that do not cohere; he recognizes the need for the right cryptographer's key, an insight equivalent to his journalist's knowledge that miraculously translates "etaoin shrdlu" from its appearance to the uninitiated as gibberish into a marking slug common to typesetting.

As Clay senses, the key lies in the Fort Worth founding of the *Globe* by Simon Bolivar Palmer, Latimer's ironic adaptation of heroic name for this patriarch, long deceased. The newspaper's move to Chicago brought along many of the Texas staff who knew Palmer, of his marriage to the present Mrs. Palmer, and of Mary Trevor (formerly Baumholtz), the ward of a music teacher named Esther Baumholtz. They also know of Simon Palmer's romance with the music teacher and his gift to her of the expensive jewelry, worth $35,000, inherited by Mary. From this, it might be reasonable to believe that Mary Trevor was Palmer's love-child, an inference seemingly denied by the report Clay receives that the girl was adopted from an Oklahoma orphanage. Mary's uncertain genealogy (for some reason she has changed her name from Baumholtz to Trevor) seems central to understanding her death.

The reporter senses the approach to truth in the fragmented ramblings of Saul Blair, a rewrite man and one of the Fort Worth veterans. Nursing a hangover, in terse clusters of nonsyntactic phrases, he tells Clay the bits and pieces he knows about Mary Trevor's life, at one point falling into gibberish induced not by poorly fitting dentures like those of the orphanage director but by his food-filled mouth: "Kibdledhertoutitoncetow." Clay's "What?" brings a translation followed by what seems a further irrelevance: "I said, I kidded her about it once, though....Mary Trevor...Larry Trevor." Sam still doesn't understand until

Blair explains that the basis of his joking with Mary Trevor lay in simply a word association from an old Country-Western song about Oklahoma bank robbers known as Larry Trevor and the Hooded Nun; the vaporous old guy quotes at length from its true-crime lyrics (69-71). As Clay discovers, the song was written by Elmo Peterkins, who also happens to be the spouse of Laura Peterkins, yet another of the *Globe* veterans and currently the editor of the society page under whom Mary Trevor worked. A sensed connectedness draws Clay forward.

As an embodiment of the slick glittery surfaces of life in modern Chicago, the *Globe* building and its higher officers make a sharp contrast to the dreamy, magical aura elsewhere appearing in manifest forms of the buried past. In *Sinners* the past continues to show itself in riddling fragments of document; when Clay comes in closest touch with the past, he is drawn by the power of its riddling, incantatory language and mythic image. Responding to Laura Peterkin's note that she must speak with him of awful knowledge she possesses, Sam visits her suburban house and feels that he has entered charmed space, a temple of the past, its forms runes of mystery:

> Circling a sprinkler on his way to the front door, Sam Clay had for the tenth time that day the feeling of being in a dream....The too-perfect grass and the trees and the monotonously whirling sprinklers made him feel alien. There was a remoteness about the yard, a timelessness, as though it had been this way—grass, trees, water, shadows and ivy—since creation and would remain so forever. As though, he thought, it had nothing to do with anything alive. (112)

Outside the house he meets Elmo Peterkins, incongruously dressed in blue-and-white striped coveralls over a dark suit, looking "like the engineer on a children's railroad." As if a dream character Elmo speaks ordinary words that nonetheless seem portentous; he directs Sam toward Laura's backyard studio, into which Elmo himself "is not permitted." Clay finds what seems prophetically fulfilled, the murdered Laura, who has been working on a wedding report for the society page in the jargon of such writing that now seems magical (114-15). In his second visit to her studio, he has an even greater sense of entering enchanted space. Elmo has chosen not to report the crime in order to contrive a ruse for drawing the murderer's return; the husband stages a seemingly revived Laura smoking a cigarette and listening to a recording of the ballad "Larry Trevor and the Hooded Nun" (191-98). Elmo's firing his rifle at a shadowy figure breaks

Clay's sense of thrall to magic; the ghost has left a deposit of real blood.

It is Clay's good fortune to have advocacy in the private detective Amos Bundy and his secretary-confidant Miss Dewhurst. Though both appear misplaced in time and space, Clay feels an immediate affinity with them; their obsolescence—their apparent emergence from the past—gives them a sorcerer's prescience and control. The British Miss Dewhurst appears to have come from an Edwardian time of mutton sleeves, straw hats, and parasols. To Clay's *thank you* her response is the Briticism Q (the sound of an abruptly bridged *thank you—kyou*); Clay decodes quickly and gives the cryptic Q back to her thenceforward, as if compatriot of spirit. The detective Amos Bundy has little interest in the spirit of modernity ("I distrust electricity.") and possesses a direct feeling for the truth in events. He is an avatar of Abraham Lincoln:

> It was a hundred-year walk from the Bundy Agency reception room, with the blond furniture, the switchboard, the electric typewriter and the automatic water-cooler to the dim interior of Mr. Bundy's office. It was a change of centuries, a trip to a museum, a visit to a certain Springfield law office. Clay, seated in a huge, springless leather chair and watching Mr. Bundy's stub pen scratch the pages of a cloth-bound ledger, felt as thought he had inadvertently wandered into the fourth dimension. (99)

On first meeting with the reporter, the Lincoln-like detective begins to restore order by decoding the signs of Clay's pocket junk and confused notes from his blackout. He organizes the searches of Tom and Camille Nichols and directs Clay in fertile directions. A master of the riddling language of events so confusing to Clay, Bundy uses riddles for their own protection because he doesn't wish for the police to intercept his message: "Cherry blossom number Yankee Lady Beaverbrook. To from airplanes fly. Already ordered cherry blossom associates kidnap mechanical man. Office twelvestroke all go well." Miss Dewhurst instinctively understands most of it: "The Washington number belongs to Mrs. Cornelia Palmer....Why it's perfectly clear. Mr. Bundy has notified his Washington operatives to kidnap the mechanical man. If they do their job he—it will be in our office at midnight" (188-89).

Though Sam Clay is certain that someone among the *Globe* managers is the assassin of Mary Trevor, their appearance of unimpeachable virtue remains their strongest defense. In contrast, Sam's reputation as a drunk makes him a likely criminal, as viewed by the editor of the religious page, Alma Plummer, who has already pieced together some of the clues suggesting that Sam was in Mary Trevor's apartment (72). Against the possible taint of scandal and criminality within the *Globe* organization, the company lawyer brings the rivalries of Canning and Standish into reconciliation for the common good of the newspaper. When he sees that Clay may be getting at the truth, Standish calls for Sam's "discretion" as "one of the family" (78-79). Latimer works comedy successfully by contrasting this fortressed credibility to the truth offered by witnesses (an elevator operator, a doorman, Patricia Bruce), all of whom back away from identifications at critical moments when they recognize they are in a den of lions. As nobodies (a kid, an African-American, a dipsomaniac woman) they know they have the least of credibility and the most to lose. Entering into his descriptions of the men who called on Mary Trevor, the elevator operator begins his sketches but with growing horror sees that the first two men he describes (Standish and Canning) stand before him and that the Sam Clay who emerges from the shadows of the room is the "murderer." Hoping to leave in safety, he offers a grossly distorted picture of the suspect as a "Great big fellow. Three hundred pounds. Beard. Long curly hair..." (81-83).

It is this wall of respectability and control that seems to make the *Globe* invulnerable. Sam Clay's list of senior staff from the Fort Worth past who have also had contact with the dead girl in Chicago grows larger. The savagery of the murder—multiple stabs and slashing, as well as the angry destruction of the girl's clothing—implies an explosion of rage in the killer, an out-of-control personality. Despite the neurotic behaviors of Standish and Canning, Sam can't think of the two as having that capacity. But his encounter with Charley Adair, who lost an arm to the war and possesses a cynical intellectual haughtiness, uncovers such a personality. Confronted with Sam's knowledge that Mary Trevor spent part of the evening of her death with Adair, the one-armed man assaults Clay, whose refusal to fight him drives the handicapped man to an even more vicious attack that ends with the use of his prosthesis "brought...around in a flat circle as though cracking a whip, and metal struck bone below Clay's temple..." (91-94). The reporter finds a similar capacity in Horace Widdecomb, Mrs. Palmer's effeminate personal assistant, whose threats and readiness to use a knife add up to the sort of imbalance that might have produced the rage seen in the murder of Mary Trevor.

On first seeing her, the reporter-detective is overwhelmed by

Cornelia Palmer's self-assured aristocratic demeanor and her mature beauty. He has already observed the anxiety of the *Globe* managers about satisfying her wishes; they are in awe if not fear of her. Her outer manner is the quintessence of their own institutional style of presumed virtue and adamantine control. In a lengthy private meeting she directly accuses Clay of the murder. Unaware that he is providing further information to the killer, Sam admits his drunken blackout and recounts his investigations into the dead woman's background. Mrs. Palmer promises him help in achieving "speedy release" if he will surrender and confess to the killing. Accepting too much of the liquor she has offered places him in his characteristic position of weakness; if the Scotch won't do it, the Luger in her hand will force him to the police. With a summoning of his reserves, he assaults her, despite her feigned sweet reasonableness ("You crazy fool!...Can't you see I'm trying to help you?"). Their fighting is genuine; her physical strength almost overpowers him; but her surrender places them in a coital position that he will not take advantage of, as she seems to understand and as a confirmation of his assertion that he could not have raped and murdered Mary Trevor (164-177).

Escaping from the Globe Tower, the reporter's certainty that either Horace Widdecomb or Cornelia Palmer has killed Mary Trevor and Laura Peterkins leads him to the bold use of the *Globe* itself to do what newspapers should do—find and speak the truth. He reenters the Globe Tower and persuades friends to accept his reset front-page story outlining his discoveries and theories. (Latimer gives us a facsimile of Clay's editing, as he does of Tom Nichols' police deposition.) The shocking release of that story pushes Mrs. Palmer to the murder of Horace Widdecomb in an effort to find another fall guy, but Clay now possesses the key that decodes all encrypted messages. As the girl who escaped the Catholic orphanage, she entered into the crime wave with Larry Trevor ending with his imprisonment but her escape. The mother of Mary Baumholtz-Trevor, she married Simon Bolivar Palmer without divorcing Larry Trevor, a fact which, if discovered, would imperil her control of Palmer Publications. Faced with threats from Mary Trevor to tell all and angered by her daughter's behaviors with Globe managers, Mrs. Palmer has murdered in rage, then sought to cover up.

The detective Amos Bundy's "mechanical man" (telephone recorder) makes it clear. Before the assembled *Globe* executives and the Chicago police, the shrilling of reversed vocatives halts. The playback offers up the decoded, identifiable voices of drunken Sam Clay and the imperial Mrs. Palmer in her daughter Mary Trevor's apartment, support for the reporter's assertion that Mrs. Palmer has flown to Chicago, murdered, and returned to Washington as alibi (240-45). Although the group's astonishment gives the woman opportunity for a temporary escape, her remorse and apparent return to the religion of her youth leads her to surrender in Holy Name Cathedral. In Clay's final musings, Jonathan Latimer brings to the narrative closure another and fuller expression of kinship as verbal motif. Thinking of the biblical metaphor of Christ as the bridegroom returned to claim the faithful, Sam Clay has "a queer feeling he was witnessing a marriage, and maybe he was. A proxy marriage with a bridegroom who'd be around later" (249). As if led away to a convent, Mrs. Palmer will seek expiation for her terrible act of child murder.

ii. *Richard Blake:*
An Un-Hooray for Hollywood
Black Is the Fashion for Dying (1959)

In *Black* the influence of Fearing's *The Big Clock* continues to be seen in Latimer's assignment of separate chapters headed by name to the perspective of individual characters: Richard Blake, Josh Gordon, Karl Fabro, Lisa Carson, etc. Like Fearing, Latimer uses the technique in order to create multiple perspectives on common events, particularly the sequence of acts in the play-within-the play leading to Caresse Garnet's murder. The shifts in perspective also provide opportunity to develop a rich sense of the circumstances and inner preoccupations of each character; the amateur detective Richard Blake does not dominate the linear plot as detective protagonists do in more traditional story. Some evidence suggests that Latimer also sought to distinguish these character voices through particularized usage and word choice; it may be to that end, for example, that a gender difference appears to be made between Richard Blake's perception of Captain Walsh's eye color as "faded burlap" and Lisa Carson's seeing them as "brown sugar" (Latimer, *Black* 85, 92).[2] In any case, Latimer's primary use of the shifts of perspective lies in the development of the mystery plot and not the painstaking representation of separate voices as in more recent mystery fiction Carl Hiaasen has done through point-of-view shifts in *Double Whammy* (1987) or Elmore Leonard in *Killshot* (1989).

Latimer establishes the pattern of the play-within-the-play in the first

chapter. Late at night the Richard Blake of *Black Is the Fashion for Dying*
is working on a hurried scene revision for the Karl Fabro production of
Tiger in the Night, an African safari movie behind schedule and over
budget. The conflicting jungle energies of characters in the movie script
seem little different from those making the movie; except for the
friendship between the director Josh Gordon, the actress Lisa Carson, and
the writer Blake, relationships on the set are marked by bitter open
hostility and private fantasies of vengeance and control. At immediate
issue is a feud between Lisa Carson and Caresse Garnet about which will
emerge the heroine in the final scene. Conceding to Caresse's demands,
Fabro has instructed Blake to revise the ending to please the aging actress.
Interruptions abound—phone calls from studio aides and a noisy car left
idling outside the writer's house. Concentration lost to the automobile, he
finds there an apparently disabled young woman in a fur coat; she is in a
comatose state, perhaps a victim of carbon monoxide. But the beautiful
blond girl is only drunk; and in Blake's efforts to awaken her with coffee,
he discovers she is nude beneath the expensive fur coat. She is, it would
seem, a failed effort on someone's part either to distract Blake from his
task or to discover the nature of his revisions.

Each associate to the making of the film *Tiger in the Night* wants its
success for the satisfaction of private desire: Karl Fabro's to seize control
of the studio from his father-in-law, Josh Gordon's to resist the producer
Fabro's cheapening of his directing standards, Caresse Garnet's to boost a
sagging career, Lisa Carson's to establish herself as a new star, Richard
Blake's to retain his comfortable status as a writer on studio contract, and
T. J. Lorrance's to maintain costly private medical treatment for his polio-
stricken daughter. Nobody wastes tears over Miss Garnet's death; several
hate her enough to murder her, either because she impedes the progress of
the film or because of the enmities she has generated over the years in
achieving and maintaining a career still of interest to such gossip
columnists as Hedda Hopper (54-55).

The scene Blake has rewritten occupies the next day's work on the
sound stage. In its prior form the half-caste native girl Ahri (Lisa) was to
murder her wealthy American rival Barbara (Caresse) for the love of the
young white hunter; then in the last scene Ahri was to give herself up "for
having done something out of primitive innocence that was morally right,
but contrary to the false laws of society." Caresse is outraged by Lisa's
being given the curtain speech and by the implication that her character

Barbara deserves execution. The revision shifts to what Blake characterizes as the "old regeneration baloney" by having Ahri only wound Barbara, who shocked to repentance gives up the young white hunter and returns to her husband (4, 5). On the set the kitsch closure begins to play itself out as Blake has redone it: unconscious from a hunting accident, Caresse as Barbara is carried into camp by bearers; Lisa as the native girl seizes a Webley pistol from its hanging holster and shoots Caresse, who (incredibly, given that she is now twice hurt) is to revive and go into her "regeneration baloney." Only problem is, she's dead, since a live bullet was somehow placed among the blanks in the Webley; and Lisa has perhaps killed (or murdered) Caresse. Or has Caresse already been murdered by someone else under cover of the sounds of hunting rifles fired by Masterton and Phelps in the progress of the scene? (55-70).

Beyond the need for answers from an autopsy, reason exists for uncertainty, since the producer Karl Fabro has required of the director Josh Gordon that the final scene be filmed using multiple cameras for different setups and perspectives through which the actors would walk without extra takes, a speeded-up process adapted from then-current television technique for the transmission of live drama. This adaptation requires a labor-intensive and frenetic synchronizing of the talents of all the actors and technicians; because each has witnessed only a special part, all are closed off from the whole sequence within which Caresse Garnet has been murdered. As Lieutenant Walsh puts it, it's as if he were investigating one of "those locked-room murders they're always putting in books" (84). Through the point-of-view shifts in separate chapters, Latimer gives us clue gathering as characters replay their part of the whole tape. Given Lisa's announced hatred of Caresse, the younger actress seems at first the most likely suspect. However, the complete sequence shown to the police and production staff makes it appear that Blake may have had opportunity to introduce a live bullet into the Webley, since the rushes show the writer responding to the director's off-camera voice calling for someone to place the gun in a better position for filming (197). Escaping from the studio, poor Blake goes on the run.

In addition to the service to the mystery plot, Latimer also uses the play-within-the-play to make thematic linkages between life and art, victim and victimizer. Victim Caresse Garnet and assassin Karl Fabro are joined in a conflict explained by the details of their vicious careerism but also by the psychologies invested in their personalities, giving their deadly encounter a dramatic inevitability. Caresse is the castrating matriarch, dangerous to sons and fathers; Karl is the Oedipal son, a danger to patriarchs and their women. In both, the fidelities of family association are dismissed by their unchecked, if not unnatural desires.

In the safari film Caresse as Barbara plays a mature, dominating woman whose marriage to the weak Phelps leads her toward seducing the young man Masterton away from a more natural, same-generation relationship with Ahri (Lisa). In the writer's life, among studio associates in varying stages of failed relationships, the divorced Blake seeks to reestablish a stable connection by marriage to Lisa Carson; it is a prospect threatened by Caresse's control of the film and himself. Latimer makes clear the Oedipal nature of Blake's fear in his repressed memories of dating the older actress, who had been like "a queen conferring favors." Blake denies having had an erotic interest in Caresse, refusing to bring to consciousness the full memory of an occasion when the word *bed* had been a subject of discussion, hoping to "shut that strange Freudian scene out of his mind" (4).

Developing her career with histrionic flair, Caresse has gone through many destructive relations, including a love affair with the poet Edgar Allan Pixley and a stormy divorce from Ashton Graves, whose traditional British acting technique makes him a displaced person in Hollywood. Losing both legs to the war, the actor has returned half-heartedly to his career but devotedly to the bottle; his flawed body is cause and sign of sexual dysfunction; and his life is, of course, the parallel to the weak spouse of Barbara (Caresse) in *Tiger in the Night.* Ashton remains in love with Caresse, who has been considering remarriage to the pathetic drunk, since he may be in line to become a baronet. Karl Fabro observes part of a surreal entertainment the actress has devised for Ashton, an evening of old films with an audience of mannequins dressed like celebrated movie personalities of the silent screen. Fabro has a sense of "The dead risen!...at a feast no sane mind could have conceived"; and when Ashton sees this life-as-movie-set he falls into raging affront since the dummies, like himself, have no legs (29, 37-38). His rage continues to boil and erupt in the play-within-the play, in which he plays the white hunter. Challenged by Josh Gordon to a sobriety test before the final scene, he enunciates carefully: "Could kill Caresse, completely compunctionless....Calumnious, carnivorous, concupiscent, consummately contemptible creature" (65).

Like Caresse, Karl Fabro is despised by all. Engaged in endless games of one-upmanship and put-down, he is nonetheless credited for his movie genius. His professional success is a complex of several causes: his power marriage to the daughter of a wealthy New York City investor, his ability to force conflicting talents toward his will, and his reputation as a writer of films that have won him an Academy Award and may possibly win another. He remains in his loveless marriage with Irene because her father Benjamin is the major investor in his studio. Karl's brilliance juggles confused shooting schedules and conflicting budgets into fruitful order through what his assistant T. J. Lorrance thinks of as a "A kind of mathematical fascism" (71). His shrewdness in saving films from disaster is legendary, exhibited here by plans to use the film footage of the dead Caresse and to negotiate with the district attorney (when Lisa Carson is briefly held as the murderer) for a promise "that the girl, if not free on bail, would be allowed to finish her scenes at the studio [since] One day's shooting and the picture would be in the can" (126). But it is Karl's writing ability that Lorrance finds most inexplicable. How can it be that behind this bullying ego and incisive brain there lurks yet a third artistic Karl capable of writing the screenplays? (77).

As Caresse Garnet knows, no such third Karl exists; his is a worst case of Hollywood exploitation of writing talent. As she knows, his scripts are plagiarized from the poetic dramas of her deceased lover, E. A. Pixley, whose originals she keeps as the basis for blackmailing Fabro into keeping her on studio contract. When his father-in-law requires the producer to fire the actress, Karl feels he has no alternative than murder. In their tracing out this inner connection between Caresse and Karl, Richard Blake and Josh Gordon find the motive of the murder. Blake's contact with the arms dealer Orthman gives him the clues by which he determines how Fabro killed Caresse and through the exchange of blank and live bullets made it appear that Lisa, then Blake himself because of his chance handling of the pistol, was guilty of the murder of Caresse.

Blake understands, now, what the dying Pixley meant by the inscription to Caresse on the poet's photograph: "Let my words rise from my ashes,/ Caresse, to sing my love!" (24). Blake devises a dramatic return from the grave of another kind to push Fabro toward breakdown or confession. Knowing that beneath the producer's outer viciousness there exists a history of mental fragility, he employs an actor to impersonate the poet Pixley on the occasion of Fabro's receiving another Oscar at the annual Academy Awards. When Kim Novak announces Fabro the winner, the producer on stage sees the reborn Pixley stand and walk the other aisle to the podium, where Karl loses composure and flees while the dead-alive poet accepts the Oscar "in the name of Edgar Allan Pixley" (211-12).

Falling into the abyss of disrepute and failure, Karl acts out ever more desperate gestures of control and rebellion against his father-in-law Benjamin, whom he hates because of the old man's continuing interference with studio policy. For some time he has hoped to wrest power from Benjamin by forcing his wife into signing over the stock her father gave her when she married Fabro; if that works, Karl will become the major stockholder in the studio. As Karl knows, Irene has fallen in love with the producer's executive assistant, T.J. Lorrance, left by his wife's decease after long illness and his daughter's polio with large medical bills. T.J. is a wimpish male retained by Karl primarily to serve as a whipping boy for the catharsis of the producer's anger; Karl can also force T.J. to do the needful dirty tricks, like stealing Pixley's play drafts from Caresse's house. The love between Irene and T.J. is rather pure, a growth of mutual pity generated by their pathetic fellow victimage. Karl forces Irene to surrender the power-of-attorney to her stock holdings and then as a sign of his contempt rapes her (190). Promising to care for T.J.'s daughter, Karl forces his assistant to sign a false confession to murdering Caresse; then preparing to murder T.J. so that the assistant's death will seem a suicide, he is stopped by the intervention of Irene. One last time, he tries to bully his way out of trouble; but Irene responds by killing him with the "automatic he had given her when they were first married" (232-37).

In this last of Jonathan Latimer's detective novels, Irene's murder of Karl Fabro is a final expression of the circularity of evil installed by the violation of kinship. Recurrently within the body of Latimer's detective fiction, violent murders are the product of sinister energies seeking to deny kinship, real or spiritual, in favor of authority and power conferred by institutions. It is a theme first coming into expression through the image of the anonymous young blond corpse of *Lady in the Morgue*. It recurs in the sacrifice of the blond sister Camelia by brother Penn in *The Dead Don't Care*, in the grotesque virgin sacrifice of Penelope Grayson by the prophet of *Solomon's Vineyard*, and in the daughter-murder of the nude blond Mary Trevor of *Sinners and Shrouds*. It is also expressed in Karl Fabro's murder of the blond prostitute he sent to determine the nature of Blake's script revisions. Despite her occupation, the writer's impression gives us another daughter-sacrifice, "a Dresden doll of a girl" of immature body looking "like a child playing grown-up in her mother's clothes" (11).

Against this victimage Latimer's detectives exerted the power of their stewardship, seeking the balance found in the closure of *Black Is the Fashion for Dying*. There, in Lisa Carson's desire to become a family with Richard Blake, to marry him "tomorrow" in order to fulfill the promise of the child she hopes she is pregnant with, the two reinstitute private kinship and private loyalties.

Notes

[1]Subsequent references in this section refer to this edition. *Sinners and Shrouds* was serialized in *Collier's* 136 (1955): 19 Aug.: 62-71; 2 S ept.: 38-53; 16 Sept.: 69-77; 30 Sept.: 84-101.

[2]Subsequent references in this section refer to this edition.

Works Cited

Novels by Jonathan Latimer

Primary:

Murder in the Madhouse. Garden City, NY: Doubleday, Doran, 1935.

Headed for a Hearse. Garden City, N.Y.: Doubleday, Doran, 1935.

The Lady in the Morgue. Garden City, N.Y.: Doubleday, Doran, 1936.

[as Peter Coffin.] *The Search for My Great-Uncle's Head.* Garden City, NY, Doubleday, Doran, 1937.

The Dead Don't Care. Garden City, NY: Double day, Doran, 1938.

Red Gardenias. Garden City, NY: Doubleday, Doran, 1939.

Solomon's Vineyard. London: Metheun, 1941.

Sinners and Shrouds. New York: Simon and Schuster, 1955.

Black Is the Fashion for Dying. New York: Random House, 1959.

Filmscripts

Year of release, title, director, studio, producer.

1939. *The Lone Wolf's Spy Hunt.* Peter Godfrey, Columbia, Joseph Sistrom.

1940. *Phantom Raiders.* Jacques Tourneur, MGM, Frederick Stephani.

1941. *Topper Returns.* Roy Del Ruth, United Artists, Hal Roach.

1941. *Night in New Orleans.* William Clemens, Paramount, Sol C. Siegel.

1942. *The Glass Key.* Stuart Heisler, Paramount, Fred Kohlmar.

1946. *Noctourne.* Edwin L. Marin, RKO, Joan Harrison.

1947. *They Won't Believe Me.* Irving Pichel, RKO, Joan Harrison.

1948. *The Big Clock.* John Farrow, Paramount, Richard Malbaum.

1948. *Beyond Glory.* John Farrow, Paramount, Robert Fellows.

1948. *The Night Has a Thousand Eyes.* John Farrow, Paramount, Endre Bohem.

1948. *The Sealed Verdict.* Lewis Allen, Paramount, Robert Fellows.

1949. *Alias Nick Beal.* John Farrow, Paramount, Endre Bohem.

1950. *Copper Canyon.* John Farrow, Paramount, Mel Epstein.

1951. *The Redhead and the Cowboy.* Leslie Fenton, Paramount, Irving Asher.

1951. *Submarine Command.* John Farrow, Paramount, Joseph Sistrom.

1953. *Botany Bay.* John Farrow, Paramount, Joseph Sistrom.

1953. *Plunder of the Sun.* John Farrow, Warner Brothers, Wayne-Fellows.

1956. *Back from Eternity.* John Farrow, RKO, John Farrow.

1957. *The Unholy Wife.* John Farrow, Universal, John Farrow.

1958. *The Whole Truth.* John Guillermin, Romulus, Jack Clayton.

Sources

Books

Baker, Carlos. *Ernest Hemingway: A Life Story.* New York: Scribner's, 1968.

Binyon, T.J. *Murder Will Out: The Detective in Fiction.* New York: Oxford, 1990.

Cain, James M. *The Postman Always Rings Twice.* New York: Knopf, 1934.

Campbell, Joseph. *The Hero with a Thousand Faces.* New York: Princeton, 1949.

Cawelti, John G. *Adventure, Mystery, and Romance.* Chicago: U of Chicago, 1976.

Cleaver, Eldridge. "The Primieval Mitosis." *Soul on Ice.* New York: McGraw, Hill, 1968.

DeAndrea, William L. Introduction. *Solomon's Vineyard.* By Jonathan Latimer. New York: International Polygonics, 1988.

Fearing, Kenneth. *The Big Clock.* New York: Harcourt, Brace, 1946.

Fogarty, Robert S. *The Righteous Remnant.* Kent, OH: Kent State, 1981.

Ford, Henry, with Samuel Crowther. *My Life and Work.* New York: Page, 1926.

Geherin, David. *The American Private Eye.* New York: Frederick Ungar, 1985.

Grella, George. "Murder and Manners: The Formal Detective Novel." *Dimensions of Detective Fiction.* Eds. Larry Landrum, Pat Browne and Ray B. Browne. Bowling Green, OH: Popular Press, 1976.

Handbook of Private Schools for American Boys and Girls. Boston: Porter Sargent, 1927.

Ickes, Harold L. *Back to Work: The Story of P.W.A.* New York: MacMillan, 1935.

Ickes, Harold L. *Secret Diary.* New York: Simon and Schuster, 1953.

Longhurst, Derek. "Sherlock Holmes: Adventures of an English Gentleman 1887-1894." London: Unwin, Hyman, 1989.

McLendon, James. *Papa: Hemingway in Key West.* Key West, FL: Langley, 1990 rev.

Moore, William T. *Dateline Chicago.* New York: Taplinger, 1973.

Murray, George. *Madhouse on Madison Street.* Chicago: Follett, 1965.

Nash, Jay Robert, and Stanley Ralph Ross, eds. *The Motion Picture Guide.* Chicago: Cinebooks, 1986.

O'Brien, Geoffrey. *Hardboiled America: The Lurid Years of Paperbacks.* New York: Von Nostrand Reinhold, 1981.

Vargas, Alberto, and Austin Reid. *Vargas.* New York: Harmony, 1978.

Variety Film Reviews 1907-1980. New York: Garland, 1983.

Veblen, Thorstein. *Theory of the Leisure Class.* New York: Viking, 1987.

West, James L.W., III. *American Authors and the Literary Marketplace since 1900.* Philadelphia: University of Pennsylvania, 1988.

Winkel, Martha G. "Georgette Heyer." *Contemporary Authors.*

Articles

Marx, Carolyn. "Book Marks." New York City *World-Telegram.* 13 Aug. 1963.

McCahery, Jim. "Jonathan Latimer's William Crane." *The Not So Private Eye.* 1 (1978), 2 (1978).

O'Grady, Judy. "The Colonel's Lady and Others." Detroit *News.* 21 Nov. 1937. Knox College Alumni Office.

Interviews

Latimer, Jonathan G. Interview by Lew Scarr. *San Diego Union* 17. June 1968: D14.

Latimer, Jonathan G. Interview by Pauline Gale. "There's Money in Mystery." *Writer* 54 (Dec. 1941).

Latimer, Jonathan W., an interview with James R. McCahery. *Megavore* 11 (Oct. 1, 1980).

Letters

Chandler, Raymond. Letter to Hamish Hamilton. 14 Feb. 1951. *Selected Letters of Raymond Chandler.* Ed. Frank McShane. New York: Columbia U, 1981.

Latimer, Jonathan G. Letter to Knox College Alumni office. 26 Nov. 1936. Knox College Alumni Office.

Latimer, Jonathan G. Letter to Knox College Alumni office. Undated. Knox College Alumni Office.

Latimer, Jonathan P. Letter to the author. 19 Mar. 1990.

Latimer, Jonathan W. "To the Editor." *Atlantic Monthly* 223 March, 1969.